Jesus the Forgiving Victim:

Listening for the Unheard Voice

Unexpected insiders

James Alison

DOERS
PUBLISHING
2624 Patriot Blvd.
Glenview, IL 60026

Jesus the Forgiving Victim website:
http://www.forgivingvictim.com
DOERS Publishing website:
http://www.doerspublishing.com
Book Design by Archer Graphics
ISBN   978-0-9818123-1-1   0-9818123-1-7

Other Books by the Author

Broken Hearts and New Creations: Intimations of a Great Reversal

Undergoing God: Dispatches from the Scene of a Break-In

On Being Liked

Faith Beyond Resentment: Fragments Catholic and Gay

The Joy of Being Wrong: Original Sin Through Easter Eyes

Raising Abel: The Recovery of the Eschatological Imagination

Knowing Jesus

Contents

BOOK ONE: *Starting human, staying human*

Essay 1   "Don't speak until you're spoken to"

Essay 2   Emmaus and Eucharist

Scriptural References

Video References

Glossary of Terms

BOOK TWO: *God, not one of the gods*

Essay 3   Who's afraid of the big bad book?
            Part One

Essay 4   Who's afraid of the big bad book?
            Part Two

Scriptural References

Video References

Glossary of Terms

BOOK THREE: *The difference Jesus makes*

Essay 5   Stand up and be godless!
          On receiving the gift of faith

Essay 6   Undergoing Atonement:
          The reverse-flow sacrifice

Essay 7   Induction into a people

Essay 8   Inhabiting texts and being discovered

Scriptural References

Video References

Glossary of Terms

BOOK FOUR: *Unexpected insiders*

Essay 9   Prayer: Getting inside the shift of desire . . 397

Essay 10   The portal and the halfway house: Spacious
           imagination and aristocratic belonging 435

Essay 11   A little family upheaval 481

Essay 12   Neighbors and insiders: What's it like to dwell
           in a non-moralistic commandment? 521

Scriptural References 565

Video References 569

Glossary of Terms 571

BOOK FOUR

ESSAY NINE

Prayer:
Getting inside the shift of desire

Introduction

Last time, as part of our exploration of what it feels like to be finding ourselves inducted into a new people, we looked at how Another other shifts us and discovers us through texts. Here, we will be continuing to explore what it is like to find ourselves on the inside of this project of being inducted, but this time by attending to how it is through learning desire that we are brought into new being. We will be looking at what is usually referred to by the term "prayer".

I'd like to start by noting something rather strange: how little there is in the New Testament on prayer. In fact, given that almsgiving, prayer and fasting are traditionally the visible pillars of what we call "religion", it is odd how little the New Testament attends to any of them. The only place where all three are treated with something like rigour is in the first eighteen verses of the sixth chapter of St Matthew's Gospel. And there they undergo, as I hope to show you, what appears to be a gross relativization. They are completely subordinated to, and reinterpreted by, a penetrating understanding of the working of desire.

It would be tempting to see this as something proper to Matthew, and so to talk about "Matthew's understanding of desire". Nevertheless the same understanding, the same intelligence of desire, can be detected at work in Luke and John as well as in St Paul. Ockham's razor would suggest that this is an intelligence that goes back to Our Lord himself. The best guide I know to laying out that intelligence and how it works is in the thought of René Girard, who has been my teacher throughout this course. So here I would like to show how Girard's thought, sometimes called mimetic theory, helps us to read these texts on prayer. You should by now be quite familiar with his approach, because I have been using it throughout this course. However, in order to remind you quite what a difference his way of thinking makes, I'll begin by giving you a comparison between his approach and a reading which depends on a folk-psychology approach to desire.

So, a brief reminder. I sometimes characterize the folk-psychology approach as the "blob and arrow" understanding of desire. In this approach, there is a blob located somewhere within each one of us and normally referred to as a "self". This more or less bloated entity is pretty stable, and there come forth from it arrows which aim at objects. So "I" desire a car, a mate, a house, a holiday, some particular clothes and so on and so forth. The desire for the object comes from the "I" which originates it, and thus the desire is authentically and truly "mine". If I desire the same thing as someone else this is either accidental and we must be rational about resolving any conflict which may arise, or it is a result of the other person imitating my desire, which is of course stronger and more authentic than their secondary and less worthy desire. Since my desiring self, my "I", is basically rational, it follows that my desires are basically rational, and thus that I am unlike those people whom I observe to have a clearly pathological pattern of desire – constantly falling for an unsuitable type of potential mate and banging their head against the consequences, or hooked on substances or patterns of behaviour that do them no good. Those people are in some way sick, and their desires escape the possibilities of rational discourse. Unlike me and my desires.

If this is an accurate understanding of how we desire, then of course the New Testament is weirdly quaint and inaccurate, for all it would be doing when talking about prayer is urging us to whip ourselves (and how can "we" whip our "selves"?) into wanting more. Furthermore, following this view the New Testament would contain within itself the seeds of the destruction of its own teaching about prayer, for in the text from St Matthew's Gospel at which we will be looking in more detail, there appears the phrase

> *When you are praying, do not heap up empty phrases as the Gentiles do; for they think that they will be heard because of their many words. Do not be like them, for your Father knows what you need before you ask him.*[1]

The logical conclusion to this, given the premise of the blob and arrow understanding of desire, is to stop praying. There is literally no point expressing your desire, since it is known independently of its expression, and its expression makes no difference at all. The New Testament text seems to be a pointer on the road towards the self-contained and religiously indifferent modern "self".

Please notice also that since desires are arrived at by the self without need of instruction or intervention from outside and don't need to be expressed in order to be real, the self-contained and self-starting "blob" with its arrows is also radically private. Part of the self-understanding of the "blob" is that it has a defensive role, protecting and hiding the "real me" and my "real desire" which is always under a certain amount of threat from the fundamentally "flaky" public world, the world of commerce, of business, of politics and of war, in which no forms of discourse are really truth-bearing. So, what I say in public, how I act in public, and what I say I want in public, are always a certain form

---

[1] Matthew 6.7–8.

of dissimulation, since it is only the private "self' which is real. And please notice how miraculously the New Testament text, once again doing itself out of a job, seems to flatter this picture of the self. For if there is one verse from this section of Matthew that almost everyone seems to remember it is where Jesus, having disparaged the attention-seeking public prayers of the Pharisees says this:

> But whenever you pray, go into your room and shut the door and pray to your Father who is in secret; and your Father who sees in secret will reward you.[2]

Behold the apparent scriptural canonization of the modern individual self (who is, of course, "spiritual", but not "religious")!

Now let's see whether we can't rescue this text from its imprisonment by the "blob and arrow" understanding of the self and learn how, rather than flattering our prejudices, it challenges us.

1. Desire according to the other

The understanding of desire which Girard has been putting forward for over half a century, and which is often referred to as "mimetic", is about as far removed from this picture as you can get. The key phrase which I never tire of repeating is "We desire according to the desire of the other." It is the social other, the social world which surrounds us, which moves us to desire, to want and to act. This doesn't sound particularly challenging when it is illus-

---

[2] Matthew 6.6.

trated in the way the entertainment industry creates celebrities, or the advertising profession manages to make particular objects or brands desirable. For few of us are so grandiose as to deny that *some* of our desires show us as being easily led and susceptible to suggestion. It becomes much more challenging when it is claimed that in fact it is not *some of our desires* that are being talked about, but the whole way in which we humans are structured by desire.

For what Girard is pointing out is that humans are those animals in which even basic biological instincts (which of course exist, and are not the same thing as desire) are run by the social other within which the instinct-bearing body is born. In fact, our capacity to receive and deal with our instincts is given to us through our being drawn towards the social other which inducts us into living as this sort of animal, by reproducing itself within us. And what makes this draw possible is the hugely developed capacity for imitation which sets our species apart from our nearest simian relatives.

Thus, to cut a long story short, recapping what we saw when we began this course: gesture, language and memory are not only things which "we" learn, as though there were an "I" that was doing the learning. Rather it is the case that, through *this body* being imitatively drawn into the life of the social other, gesture, language and memory form an "I" that is in fact one of the symptoms, one of the epiphenomena, of that social other. This "I" is much more highly malleable than it is comfortable to admit. And even more difficult: it is not the "I" that has desires, it is desire that forms and sustains the "I". The "I" is something like a snapshot in time of the relationships which pre-exist it and one of whose symptoms it is.

This picture is severely unflattering in that it seems to un-anchor the "I" from a cosily sacred certainty of being "something basically good in the midst of a somewhat 'iffy' world". Instead it points out that it is not so much that we are afloat on a dangerous sea, as that we are the dangerous sea we are afloat on. Our economic systems, our military conflicts, our erotic life, our ways of keeping law and order, are all part of each other, run by the same patterns of desire. Or, in other words, we humans are not only slightly affected by, but are actually run by, a culture of war and of violence. We are found as the species which acts in groups to grab at identity "over against" some conveniently designated other; and which relies on a violent contrast in order to survive, and to define value and forge culture.

As you can imagine, prayer is going to look somewhat different if this is the sort of animal who is to be doing the praying. Because in this picture, prayer is going to start from the presupposition that we all desire according to the desire of the other. It is going to raise the question: Yes, but which other? We know there is a *social* other which gives us desire and moves us this way and that. But is there *Another other*, who is not part of the social other, and who has an entirely different pattern of desire into which it is seeking to induct us? That, as we have seen, is the great Hebrew question, the discovery of God who is not-one-of-the-gods, and our texts on prayer are part of our way into becoming part of the great Hebrew answer.

2. Which other?

So thoroughly do we assume the "blob and arrow" model of self and desire that we find it difficult to imagine that the New Testament authors might be closer to the world of what we would consider primitive animist cults than to our own. For in the world of animist cults it is perfectly obvious to everybody that people are moved by what is other than themselves. Indeed, in the various trances or dances into which the participants are inducted by mixtures of music and chanting, "spirits" will "come down" and "possess" or "ride" the participants, whose normal demeanour will be temporarily displaced by the quite recognizable public persona of the spirit in question.

Given this, it is perhaps interesting to see how much closer to that world St Paul is than we sometimes imagine:

> *We know that the whole creation has been groaning in labor pains until now; and not only the creation, but we ourselves, who have the first fruits of the Spirit, groan inwardly while we wait for adoption, the redemption of our bodies. For in hope we were saved. Now hope that is seen is not hope. For who hopes for what is seen? But if we hope for*

what we do not see, we wait for it with patience.
Likewise the Spirit helps us in our weakness; for
we do not know how to pray as we ought, but that
very Spirit intercedes with sighs too deep for words.
And God, who searches the heart, knows what is
the mind of the Spirit, because the Spirit inter-
cedes for the saints according to the will of God.[3]

To paraphrase: "We are part of a new social other that is being brought into being, painfully, in the midst of the collapse of a dead-end way of being human. This new social other is being brought into being through our learning to desire it, which is something we want, but are very poor at articulating. The tension of being pulled between two sorts of social other is absolutely vital for us – and what enables us to live it is hope. Given that we don't know how to desire and express our desire, the Spirit is Another other desiring within us without displacing us so that it will actually be we who are brought into the New Creation."

Please see what Paul and the animists have in common: the understanding that we are more desired-in than desirers. And that this is, in itself, neither a good nor a bad thing. It is just what we are. The difference between the animists and the Hebrew question is not *whether* we are moved by another, but *by which other* are we moved? For "spirits", idols and so forth are merely violent disguises by which the social other moves us, such that those spirits temporarily displace us, make us act "out of character" and trap us into being functions of themselves, usually

---

[3] Romans 8.22–27.

demanding sacrifice. Whereas the Spirit of God is the Spirit of the Creator, and thus is in no way at all a function of anything that is. Quite the reverse, everything that is is a function of the Creator. The Creator is not in any sort of rivalry with us, and is thus able to move us from within, bringing us into being, without displacing us.

Let us not be fooled by a difference of language here: traditionally we refer to spirits *possessing* people, and there is, in the word "possess", a note of violence concerning the relationship between the spirit and the person possessed. When it comes to the Holy Spirit, we refer to the Spirit *indwelling*, or inhabiting the person, words without any connotation of violence. However, please notice that the human mechanism of being moved is the same in both cases. What is different is the quality of the "other" that is doing the moving.

I hope that we are now in a better position to look at some of the Gospel texts on prayer.

3. The public nature of desire

The first thing I want to point out about them is that they take for granted the public nature of human life and relationships including prayer. As one would expect, given the understanding of desire which I've been trying to flesh out with you, it is not the case that there are two equal and opposed realities: who I am in public and who I am in private. Rather it is the case that there is one reality: who I am in public. Privacy is a temporary abstraction from an essentially public way of being. Jesus, and the New Testament as a whole, simply takes for granted the public nature of religious, cultural and political life. Given that, it becomes more plausible to see why Jesus is described in various places as withdrawing to pray. Typically these moments of withdrawal come in the immediate aftermath of a major interaction with a crowd following a miracle. And it is not hard to see why. The risk which any leader runs, especially one who is enjoying a certain success, is becoming infected by the desires of their followers, allowing themselves to believe about themselves what the followers believe, and to be flattered into acting out the projections which have raised them up, and thus to become the puppet of their crowd's desires.

Jesus' moving off to pray shows that he understood his need to detox from the pattern of desire which threatened to run him – people wanting to make him King, or proclaim him as Messiah in a way that was far from what he was trying to teach them. He was acquainted with what we call temptation – the risk of being lured by the social other into a pattern of desire which is presented under the guise of being good but is not good. So, he needed to spend time having his "I" strengthened by receiving his pattern of desire from Another other. One classic recognition of Jesus' being tempted, and his refusal to be beguiled by it, comes when he tells Peter "Get thou behind me, Satan!"[4]

---

[4] Mark 8.33.

He rejects Peter's attempt to dissuade him from entering into the pathway of suffering that will lead to his death. Peter is linked to the Tempter, the stumbling block, and is told that his mind is disposed according to the culture of men, and not according to the culture of God.

Given this, let us turn to Jesus' explicit teaching about prayer, especially as we find it in Matthew 6, but with some reference to Luke also.

The first thing we notice is that Jesus' comments on prayer are embedded in a teaching about patterns of desire.

> *"Beware of practicing your piety before others **in order to be seen by them**; for then you have no reward from your Father in heaven. So whenever you give alms, do not sound a trumpet before you, as the hypocrites do in the synagogues and in the streets, **so that they may be praised by others**. Truly I tell you, they have received their reward. But when you give alms, do not let your left hand know what your right hand is doing, so that your alms may be done in secret; and your Father who sees in secret will reward you."* [5] (emphasis mine)

Before he gets to talking about prayer, Jesus is already demonstrating an understanding of desire. His presupposition is that we are all immensely needy people who long for approval and rewards. He doesn't say "Really, this is too infantile. You shouldn't be wanting approval or rewards. Grow up and be self-starting, self-contained heroic individ-

---

[5] Matthew 6.1–4.

uals who act on entirely rational grounds." On the contrary, he takes it for granted that we desperately need approval. The question is: whose approval is going to run us? The danger of seeking approval from the social other is that you will get it, and thereafter you will be hooked on that approval. It will literally give you to be who you are and what you will become. You will act out of the pattern of desire which the social other gives you.

I used to think that the phrase "Truly I tell you, they have received their reward", especially when pronounced in booming tones by a Scots-accented Calvinist preacher, was a euphemism for sending someone to hell. But it makes much more sense if you see it as an anthropological observation: the trouble about seeking the approval of the social other is that you will get it! You will act in such a way as to get that approval, and then become its puppet. And because of that you will be selling yourself short. You won't be wanting enough, you will have too little desire. Your "self" will be a shadow of what you could be if you allowed the Creator to call you into being.

(As an aside: isn't it interesting that Jesus' example of how one should give alms is physiologically almost impossible. What on earth does it mean, in practice, for the left hand not to know what the right hand is doing? It suggests the kind of lack of personal coordination that only a person who isn't a stable self can manage. I'm not quite sure what is being recommended here, but I got a hint of what it might mean not long ago. After some time of going along with the seemingly endless requests for money from a friend whom I had been supporting, I was tempted to do some accounting and work out how much I had given him over time as part of a way of trying to put some parameters into place as to what my giving and our relationship might look like in the future. Mercifully I'm not a very good accountant, but in any case, halfway through my record-checking exercise, I realized that I was, as it were, grasping onto my own generosity, attempting to make of it something that defined me over against him, in such a way that it became a bargaining chip in a relationship. And I also realized that in that very moment of grasping, what I had been doing had ceased to be an act of generosity, and I had ceased to be someone through whom Another other's generosity might flow.)

When Jesus turns to prayer the understanding of desire is identical: what people really want is approval, a particular reputation in the eyes of others and this leads them to act out in such a way that they will get that approval – and that is the problem. They get the approval, and with it, they are given a "self" that is the function of the group's desire. Belonging and approval go together. This means, incidentally, that someone is thereafter exceedingly unlikely to be self-critical in relationship to their group belonging. They will agree to cover up whatever in themselves and in other group members needs covering up in order for the group to maintain its unanimity, and for themselves to keep their reputation, which means their "self".

> "And whenever you pray, do not be like the hyp-
> ocrites; for they love to stand and pray in the syn-
> agogues and at the street corners, so that they may
> be seen by others. Truly I tell you, they have
> received their reward. But whenever you pray, go
> into your room and shut the door and pray to your
> Father who is in secret; and your Father who sees
> in secret will reward you."[6]

Instead Jesus urges his disciples to receive their "self" from "Another other" (and the Matthean code for "Another other" is "your Father who sees in secret" or "your Father who is in heaven" – that is, the Creator who is absolutely not part of the give and take, the tit-for-tat reciprocity of the social other). The image Jesus uses here is curious, since mostly our translations refer to a "room" into which we are supposed to go, which we in turn tend to associate with our bedroom, assuming that to be a private place. Yet the word ταμεῖον is more accurately rendered "storeroom", larder or pantry. This was the room, in an ancient Middle Eastern house, which was totally enclosed inside a building, with no windows. The purpose of such a space in a culture which had neither central heating nor refrigeration was to ensure that perishable food stored in it would be less susceptible to extremes of either cold or heat. It also meant that once you had shut the door from the inside, you could neither see out, nor be seen.

---

[6] Matthew 6.5–6.

Here in short, Jesus is recommending the psychological equivalent of the physiological dislocation we saw in the previous example. He is saying: "You are addicted to being who you are in the eyes of your adoring public, or your execrating public, it doesn't matter which, since crowd love and crowd hate give identity in just the same dangerous way. So, go into a place where you are forcibly in detox from the regard of those who give you identity so that your Father, who alone is not part of that give and take, can have a chance to call your identity into being."

4. The interface of desire and voices

Now here's the trouble with spending time in the larder, removed from the eyes of your public, unable to act out. You gradually start to lose "who you are". You start to dwell in the strange place which I call the interface between your "own" desire, very small, and only tentatively coming into being, timidly and somewhat shamefacedly, and the voices which run you, and which you have in fact so perfectly ventriloquized. I presume I'm not unique in having, after some time spent alone, occasionally detected the person who was speaking through me – the voice of my father or mother, or a headmaster, or some admired teacher, or political or religious leader. In other words, I had been giving voice to a pattern of desire taken on board from someone else. And of course, doing it with all the conviction of it being really *me* who was talking and desiring.

And that can be quite a shocking moment, as I realize how easily I have allowed myself to put aside, and indeed even to trample on, whatever delicate hints were pulling me in other less strident directions, and have instead rushed headlong into the first "persona" that seemed to give me a chance of being someone who counts. It is only with time spent in the larder that I may find that the One who sees me in secret is actually calling forth a quite different and richer set of desires, without such an easy and narrow straitjacket as my current persona. Furthermore, the One who sees in secret seems to be in much less of a hurry for me to avoid shame and "measure up" than I normally am.

Imagine, if you will, a childhood scene. Little Johnny is about to go to bed. A parent comes to tuck him in and says "Little Johnny, did you say your prayers?" "Yes I did." "Good, little Johnny. And what did you ask for in your prayers?" "I asked for … chocolate pudding tomorrow and for Arsenal to win on Saturday." "Oh no, little Johnny, you shouldn't ask for chocolate pudding tomorrow and for Arsenal to win on Saturday. You should be praying for an end to suffering in the Middle East, relief for the famine in Bangladesh and the Holy Father's Mission intentions for the month of May!" Well, of course, little Johnny will take this on board. His smelly little desires have been treated with contempt, and he has been taught to despise them and instead to want much more "noble" things, things that will make him stand tall in the world of his parents. In fact, he has been taught St Matthew's Gospel in reverse: desire according to the social other so as to get approval.

Here's the thing: little Johnny is fast on the road to becoming a perfect puritan, a dweller in a world in which there are things that are nice but naughty, things one wants but shouldn't say so, but also a world in which there are things which are good but boring, which one doesn't really want, but should at least say one does.

The curious thing is that, if we are to believe the Gospel, this is the reverse pattern of what God wants. It would appear that "Your Father who sees in secret" doesn't despise our smelly little desires, and in fact, suggests that if only we can hold on to them, and insist on articulating them, that we will actually find for ourselves, over time, that we want more than those desires, but we really do want something with a passion. In other words, he takes us seriously in our weakness and unimportance, even when we don't. If we learn to give some voice to those desires, then there's a chance over time that we may move through them organically until we find ourselves the sort of humungous desirers who throw ourselves into peace work in the Middle East, or into famine relief in Bangladesh, or even into being the sort of missionary for whom the Holy Father wants people to pray in May. But we'll be doing so because we, who start from not really knowing what we want, by not despising our little desires, and learning to articulate them, have discovered from within that this is what we really want. And in our wanting will be who we come to be.

5. The importunate widow

Before returning to our Matthew text, let me give a couple of further examples of the pattern of desire the Gospel texts on prayer point to, for they fit well into this larder or pantry where we find ourselves dwelling in the interface between our desires and our internal "voices" – the voices of the social other which we have internalized. Here is the model whom Jesus puts before us for prayer in Luke's Gospel: an importunate widow.[7]

> *Then Jesus told them a parable about their need to pray always and not to lose heart.*

OK, hold that thought. At first blush this sounds as though Jesus is giving advice about not becoming discouraged. I want to suggest that it is rather more than that. It is about how, through becoming insistent desirers, we will actually be given a heart, be given to be. If we do not desire, we will not have a heart.

> *He said, "In a certain city there was a judge who neither feared God nor had respect for people."*

Please notice that this judge is a perfectly non-mimetic person. In fact he is more like a concrete block than like a person, since he is able to be moved neither by the social other, nor the Other other.

---

[7] Luke 18.1–8.

> *In that city there was a widow who kept coming to him and saying, 'Grant me justice against my opponent.'*

Now we have an inconvenient person, the sort of person who has no one to stand up for her, who is not held in high regard, and whose satisfaction is of no importance to those living in the city. In her extreme vulnerability she is the equivalent of little Johnny's smelly desire. But she is persistent, and just keeps on with her demand.

> *For a while he refused; but later he said to himself, 'Though I have no fear of God and no respect for anyone, yet because this widow keeps bothering me, I will grant her justice, so that she may not wear me out by continually coming.'"*

The judge has an enviable degree of self-knowledge, for he understands perfectly well that he is a concrete block, hermetically sealed from mimetic influence. Even so, he eventually concedes, anxious to avoid a drubbing at the hands of this redoubtable widow. I say "drubbing", for the word ὑπωπιάζῃ, which we translate as "wear out", was apparently the language of the wrestling arena or the boxing ring.

> *And the Lord said, "Listen to what the unjust judge says. And will not God grant justice to his chosen ones who cry to him day and night?*

Does Jesus really think that God is like an unjust judge? Indeed not. But he knows how all of us are inclined to have an unjust judge well installed into our consciousness. In

416

fact as part of our socialization we acquire a voice or set of voices which seem to be completely impervious to anything. This voice or voices, should we be so bold as to want something, will quickly send down little messages to us: "Shouldn't want that if I were you – better not to want much, so as not to be disappointed", or "Getting above our station are we?" or, as in the famous Oliver Twist scene, "More?!!" And the point of these messages is to shut down our desire – to get us to mask our discontent with remaining mere puppets of our group. Our unjust judge is internal to each one of us, a glowering "no" in the face of our potential happiness.

Yet what Jesus recommends is a long-running, persistent refusal to have our smelly little desires put down. Instead we are to engage in a constant guerrilla warfare of desiring, so that eventually even the block in our head starts to yield, and what is right for us starts to become imaginable and obtainable. God is not like the judge, a hermetic block, he is like the irritating desire which gets stronger and stronger. It is only through our wanting something that God is able to give it to us.

> Will he delay long in helping them? I tell you, he will quickly grant justice to them. And yet, when the Son of Man comes, will he find faith on earth?"

Curiously, at the end of this teaching Our Lord shows a certain ambivalence about us. Imagination and desire feed each other positively, and this is a vital element of faith:

becoming able to imagine something good, and so to want it, and then as one wants it more, finding it more possible to imagine it more fully. Here he seems aware that despite what he is attempting to implode in our midst, we are frighteningly likely to be content with far too little, to go along with our internalized unjust judges, and so not to dare to imagine a goodness which could be ours, and thus not dare to want it, let alone become crazed single-minded athletes of system-shattering desire. He wonders whether we will really allow ourselves to be given heart.

Before moving along from this image, I'd like to point out an important part of the way the new "self" of desire is brought into being. That is by *saying* "I want". Please notice that this simple act of *saying* something, and in fact saying it frequently, is much more important psychologically than it seems. For it is not that there is an "I" that has such and such a desire, which it is now expressing. Rather, among the patterns of desire which are running this body, this body is having the humility to recognize that it needs to be brought into being by being directed in a certain way, and so is, as it were, making an act of commitment to a certain sort of becoming. "I want such and such" is an act of commitment to be found in a certain becoming, an act of alignment. "I" am agreeing that in my malleability, the desire according to the other, which precedes me, and which I'm agreeing to take on board, will bring me into being. Language makes this public, which is why it can be such a relief finally to be able to say "I want such and such", even "privately", because saying it has involved me in getting over the shame of being found to be the sort of person who wants such a thing.

A couple of final examples of the Gospel teaching the same pattern of desire as regards prayer. In Luke 6.28 we read:

> "Bless those who curse you, pray for those who abuse you."

I hope it now makes much more sense why this is emphatically not a way of saying "Jesus wants me as a doormat." On the contrary. Jesus knows very well how we become intimately involved with that subsection of the social other which are our enemies in just the same way as we become intimately involved with those whose approval we seek. He knows how susceptible we are to taking our enemies on board, and becoming just like them by acting out reciprocally towards them. So he offers us this recipe for freedom: do not allow yourselves to be run by those who do you evil. This involves a refusal of negative reciprocity and a learning to move from the heart towards them in a way which has nothing to do with what they have done to you. In fact he is saying "step out of the pattern of desire in which you are enthralled by, and in thrall to, your enemies, and step arduously instead into a pattern of desire such that you are not over against them at all, but are able to be, as God is, *for* them, towards them, without being their rival."

In case you think I'm making this up, Matthew's version of the same saying is perfectly instructive:

> But I say to you, Love your enemies and pray for those who persecute you, **so that you may be children of your Father in heaven; for he makes his sun rise on the evil and on the good, and sends rain on the righteous and on the unrighteous.** [8]
> (emphasis mine)

The rationale for praying for those who persecute you is set out clearly: it is so as to become part of the pattern of desire of the Other other, who is not part of the reciprocity, the tit for tat, the good and evil of the social other, but is entirely outside it, not in rivalry with it, and perfectly generous towards it.

6. Seeing myself through the eye of Another

Let us step back now, into our larder or pantry, to consider further the oddity of this place of the interface between our desire and the voices which run us. So far I've emphasized the negative – the rupture – what we are becoming dislocated from – the way we have been run by the regard of the social other. Now please note that there is no alternative to being run by the regard of another. It is not the case that we can strip off the false selves given us by the social other, and that there, underneath it all, radiantly, will be our true self, untrammelled by the social other.

No, we always receive ourselves through the eye of another. The really hard matter of prayer is learning to

---

[8] Matthew 5.44–45.

receive ourselves through the eye of Another other. For
what on earth is it like to be looked at by Another other?
What does that "regard" tell us of who we are, and who we
are becoming?

My sense is that the collapse of the "self of desire"
which begins when we step temporarily out of the regard
of the social other is much easier to notice than the much
quieter and more imperceptible calling into being of a new
self-of-desire, without any flashy over-againsts, or bits of
grasped self, sodden with the wrong sorts of meaning. But
it is here that the work of imagination, to which Jesus was
appealing in his example of the importunate widow, has its
proper place. For it is as we stretch the boundaries of our
imagination formed by the social other that we may catch
glimpses of being looked at by One who is not part of that
at all.

What, for instance, is meant by the *deathlessness* of
God? And here, I don't mean the usual associations which
come with "immortality" or "eternity" – meaning something like invulnerabililty, or going on for an awfully long
time. Rather, part of what we mean when we talk about
being looked at by God is that we are held in the regard of
someone who is ἀθάνατος – deathless. Someone for whom,
unlike anyone we know or have ever known, death is not a
parameter, a reality, a limit, a circumscription. Someone,
therefore, for whom mortality, existence in limited time,
our reality, looks entirely different. Someone who can wish

us into acting as if death were not. This is the sort of regard that can suggest into us the possibility of believing it is worthwhile to undertake projects whose fruition we may not see. The sort of regard that is unhurried enough not to be bothered by my failure, that empowers me to share the space of those who are despised because secure about my long-term prospects. It is the sort of regard for whom Keynes's famous phrase "in the long term, we're all dead" is simply meaningless, for the only long term that exists is one in which death has no incidence.

Or again, what does it mean to be looked at through eyes that only know *abundance*, for whom scarcity is simply not a reality, for whom there is always more? Think of the rupture this produces in my patterns of desire! "If you want more, there won't be enough to go round", or "There's no free meal at the end of the universe", or "Grab what you can before it all runs out", or just the gloomy depressed "euugh" of disappointment with things, life, and so on not matching up to expectation, the way of being in the world and perceiving everything which the ancient Hebrews referred to as vanity, or futility. What does it look like to spend time in the regard of One for whom it is not, as the whole of our capitalist system presupposes, scarcity that leads to abundance by promoting rivalry, which we then bless and call competition? Rather it is a hugely leisured creative abundance that is the underlying reality, and an endless *magis*, "more", is always on the way.

What does it look like to spend time in the regard of one for whom *daring* and adventure, not fear and caution, underlie the whole project of creation, for whom everything that *is* is open-ended and pointing to more than itself, and for whom we are invited to share in the Other's excitement and thrill, to want and to achieve crazy and unimaginable things?

What is it like to sit in a regard which is bellowing at us "something out of nothing, something out of nothing"? Our pattern of desire says "Unnhh, nothing comes from nothing" and feels sorry for itself. Yet the heart of the difference between atheism and belief in God-who-is-not-one-of-the-gods is not an ideology, but a pattern of desire which thrills to "something out of nothing". The wonderful verses of Second Isaiah, fresh from the great breakthrough into monotheism in the sixth century BC shout this out:[9]

> *Ho, everyone who thirsts, come to the waters; and you that have no money, come, buy and eat! Come, buy wine and milk without money and without price. Why do you spend your money for that which is not bread, and your labor for that which does not satisfy? Listen carefully to me, and eat what is good, and delight yourselves in rich food. Incline your ear, and come to me; listen, so that you may live. I will make with you an everlasting covenant, my steadfast, sure love for David.*

This is a definition of God as quite outside the pattern

---

[9] Isaiah 55.1–3.

of desire into which the social other inculcates us: "something out of nothing".

Well, these terms – deathlessness, abundance, daring and something out of nothing – are just a few of the sorts of phrase by which the Scriptures attempt to nudge our imagination into spending time undergoing a regard that is not the regard of the social other, one which has a wish, a longing, a heart that is *for* us, much more for us than we are for ourselves, one which we can trust to have our long-term interests at heart. And in each case, spending time in the regard of the Other other will work to produce in us a way of being public which seems to go directly counter to the expectations of the patterns of desire which the social other produces in us. Our temporary abstraction from public life will not have made us private. It will have empowered us to be public in a new way, whose precariousness and vulnerability rests on an unimaginable security.

7. Not leaving Las Vegas

Let us get back then, finally, to Matthew and the conclusion of Jesus' remarks about prayer. I hope that they will read somewhat differently now:

> "When you are praying, do not heap up empty phrases as the Gentiles do; for they think that they will be heard because of their many words. Do not be like them, for your Father knows what you need before you ask him."[10]

---

[10] Matthew 6.7–8.

I remember standing on a hill overlooking Lake Titicaca and watching the local Yatiris, shamans or priests, plying their wares. You could go to them, and for an appropriate offering, they would then light candles around little portable shrines, burn incense, and say the requisite prayers or incantations, which were in an amazing mixture of Latin, Quechua, Aymara and Spanish. The prayers or incantations were for a fairly repetitive list of things: protection from a neighbour's evil eye, quick riches, death of a troublesome mother-in-law, to get an unwilling prospective love-match to fall for me, various forms of vengeance.

The pattern seemed to be simple: God, or the gods, are a sort of celestial Las Vegas slot machine, full of amazing bounty, but inclined to be retentive. So prayer is the art of conjuring this capricious divinity, by exactly the right phrases, repeated exactly the right number of times, into parting with some of its treasure. As if the priest were a particularly expert puller of the slot-machine handle, one who could ensure that three lemons, or five bars, line up and so manipulate the divinity into disgorging its riches.

What this presupposes is a pattern of desire where we are subjects who are in control, and God is an object who must be manipulated: we are back to the blob and arrow picture of desire. What Jesus is teaching is exactly the reverse of this. In Jesus' picture it is God who is the subject, who has a desire, an intention, a longing, and who knows who we are and what is good for us; and we who are capricious and somewhat inert slot machines who are always getting our handles pulled by the wrong players. In this picture it is precisely because our Father knows what we need before we ask him that we must learn to pray: our Father's only access to us, the only way he can get to our slot-machine handle, is by our asking him into our pattern of desire.

You remember that with the blob-and-arrow understanding of desire, Jesus' phrase about "your Father knows what you need before you ask him" works as a way of making prayer pointless. But with the mimetic understanding of desire which I hope to have shown to be at work throughout this passage, the same phrase works in exactly the opposite way. It becomes the urgent reason why we need to pray: so as to allow the One who knows what is good for us, unlike us ourselves, whose desire is for us and for our fruition, unlike the social other and its violent traps, to gain access to re-creating us from within, to giving us a "self", an "I of desire" that is in fact a constant flow of treasure. We are asking, in fact to become a symptom of his pattern of desire, rather than that of the social other which ties us up into becoming so much less.

8. The Our Father

It is with this then, that Jesus leads up to teaching the "Our Father".

"Pray then in this way: Our Father in heaven, hal-

lowed be your name. Your kingdom come. Your will be done, on earth as it is in heaven. Give us this day our daily bread. And forgive us our debts, as we also have forgiven our debtors. And do not bring us to the time of trial, but rescue us from the evil one. For if you forgive others their trespasses, your heavenly Father will also forgive you; but if you do not forgive others, neither will your Father forgive your trespasses."[11]

Before we go into a line-by-line reading of this, I'd like to ask you to imagine yourself not as standing stably on a firm surface, being instructed about words to say; rather, imagine yourself as highly malleable, being stretched between two force fields, two patterns of desire. What the "Our Father" is doing is inducting you into a pattern of desire within which you may be found, one which will enable you to inhabit the "being stretched" which is how the desire of the Other other brings into being the daughter or son who is learning to pray.

So, line by line:

"Our Father in heaven,

Here, entirely without rivalry with anything that is, in no way part of the push and pull, the tit for tat of human togetherness, is the Other other. But not merely Other in a distant and removed way: Father, one who is for us, below us, young and excited about who we might come to be, the very ground of possible familiarity, the guarantor that prior to any of our fear, resentment and shame at our-

---

[11] Matthew 6.9–15.

selves and each other there is a way for us to be sisters and brothers that will be a delight to us.

hallowed be your name.

Most special invocation of the stretched-between world! You remember how God gave himself a non-name Name for Moses, and how Jesus' acting out in going to the cross was so that he would be given the Name that is above every other name? So here we are being urged to desire "Cause your reputation, your personality, who you are really like, to become visible, detectable, reverenceable in our midst." Anything more solid than the Name of the Holy One, a constantly flickering hologram of revelation, would quickly become an idol that we could grasp. Anything less visible, less capable of being sensed and reverenced would leave us without hints that this world is one which is marked, loved, projected, owned; and we would be left adrift in the huge impersonality of an un-owned universe. So part of how we find ourselves is in the longing to see the visible signs in our midst of the personal, named, directed, ownership of everything that is.

Your kingdom come.

The project which the Other other has is already on the way. All that realization, that fruition, that effective and purposeful building up of something that is to be, one which doesn't know shading down into futility, disappointment and abandonment: all that is the sign of a Kingship quite unlike anything that we can imagine while borrowing the terminology derived from "glorious rulers" here on earth, and it presupposes a pattern of desire quite unlike anything we are used to, one which is way prior to any pattern of desire we know, and yet which can move us to want and to create hints of that Kingdom now. So we need to be inducted into wanting it. Being on the inside of it means having our pattern of desire re-created so that we become the project's conscious agents:

Your will be done, on earth as it is in heaven.

So, may Your pattern of desire be achieved, here in our midst, amongst all these things that we are so often quick to reject, to despise, to tire of, be bored of, made to despair by. Your pattern of desire which already has and is a huge rejoicing and delight, a huge benevolence and peaceful longing, a real reality upon which our small reality rests, and from which it so often seeks to cut itself off, incapable of perceiving itself as the symptom of so much glory. May we be taken onto the inside of this pattern of desire. Remind us that we are the slot machine, and you the delighted player, so happy and lucky to have found us, fine-tuning us into disgorging far more treasure than we ever knew we had.

Give us this day our daily bread.

I think there are two references here: the people of Israel were told to gather manna in the desert, but only what was sufficient for the day, not to collect more, to store or to save, except on the eve of the Sabbath, when they could collect for two days. This too is a teaching about desire: those who know they are loved don't need to be anxious for more, but can relax into knowing that they can ask for and will be given what they need by someone who knows their needs more than they do themselves. So, day by day to be able to learn to trust the goodness of the giver is a constant shift in our pattern of desire.

However, just as longing for God to cause his Name to pulsate in our midst, even in the circumstances of this earth, is part of opening up our pattern of desire, so too is the longing for the bread of heaven, the food which deepens hunger even as it satisfies it. I think the reference here is to the Blessed Bread in the Temple, understood to be the sign coming down into our midst of the one who longs for us to want more, to eat more, in a way which pulls us right out of our smaller wantings and cravings. For us who are living the Temple as the Body of Christ, it is the Eucharist, like the Name, suspended midway between this world and the one which is breaking in, which symbolizes and makes present a simultaneous deepening and satisfying of desire which draws us on.

> *And forgive us our debts, as we also have forgiven our debtors.*

Surprise surprise: Our Lord takes for granted the fact that we are entirely mimetic animals. It is only in our letting go of the "social other" that we can find ourselves let go. It is as we find ourselves being able to unbind others, let them go, rather than being tied in to them with ever tighter violent reciprocity, that we find ourselves being let go, and in finding ourselves being let go, actually find ourselves. Who we are is formed relationally, and it is strictly in our relation with what is other than us that we will be found to be.

And do not bring us to the time of trial,

Once again, think yourself inside the pattern of desire which we are being asked to inhabit. One of the ways we avoid trusting someone who likes us is to hold them at a distance by considering that maybe they are capricious, maybe they have hidden intentions, and that maybe they are leading us in a particular way just to test us – not because it is good for us, but because we are playthings, and it is good for them. And in fact, as humans we are surrounded by a social other that treats us in just such ways. Part of learning that the Other other is not part of the social other at all is learning that there are no hidden intentions in God, the Other other is totally *for us*, we can allow the Other other to take over our whole heart without fear. We don't need to hold back a tiny bit so as to take an "adult" distance, second-guessing his project for us.

Linked to this is our tendency to want to grasp identity through the excitement of a challenge: it seems so exciting to grasp at identity by comparison with some convenient other over against whom I can become a hero, or a victim, it doesn't really matter which. In either case at least I get to be, have an identity, however much of a junk identity it turns out to be. So much more exciting than agreeing to the slow business of being given an identity as a daughter or son of God, without any "over against"! Yet this need for identity by grabbing for a quick fix masks a despair about there being any real "me" that is being called into existence over time. So here we are inducted into a pattern of desiring whereby we agree to lose the quick-fix identities we might grab through "tests" so as to be given something much richer and deeper which will hold us up, but which we cannot grab.

But rescue us from the evil one.

Continuing with the same pattern of desire, Our Lord situates us with relation to what is evil. There is nothing evil in God, and any attribution of evil to God works as a way of our preventing ourselves from trusting God whole-heartedly. If God is two-faced, Janus, we will always be shadow-boxing, never allowing ourselves to be indwelt. That which is evil is real, but we are not to seek it out, face it down – the thing about evil is that the more we try to define it and face it, the more real it gets, and the more we become it. Think how easily people get fixated on their enemies, and then, without realizing it, become more and more like them, until they are mirror images of each other. The pattern of desire into which we are being inducted by the Lord's Prayer recognizes evil, but only as that from which people can be delivered. Rather than its being a thing in itself, it is only known in its being left behind to curve down on itself, never to be given oxygen by being dignified with a concentrated gaze. But the real force in the universe is not evil, but love, and love really does want to rescue us, to bring us out of our tendency to enclose ourselves in smaller and smaller spaces, to bring us into being.

And then finally:

> For if you forgive others their trespasses, your heavenly Father will also forgive you; but if you do not forgive others, neither will your Father forgive your trespasses."

The one section of the pattern of desire which our Lord repeats and emphasizes is the central anthropological point around which the whole of his teaching has been built: it is in our letting go of the social other that we find ourselves let go by the Other other. This is the shape of our being stretched into being.

I hope you will agree, then, that "desire according to the desire of the other", and the absolute and mechanical mimetic working of our desire, do not seem to be foreign imports into these texts on prayer, but to offer a rich reading of them that goes with their flow. May they help us to be found on the inside of the adventure of prayer as part of the shift by which we are inducted into a new people.

The portal and the halfway house:

Spacious imagination and aristocratic belonging

Introduction

I f you're anything like me, you have been wondering, as we have advanced in our course, how what we've been looking at bears any relation at all to "life in the Church" as we know it. The forms of institutional life called "Church" with which we are familiar, either from personal experience or by hearsay, seem far removed from what I have been trying to open up for you: how the crucified and risen Jesus interacts with his disciples in such a way as to induct us into a new people no longer run by fear of death. I know it's a tall order, but here I'm going to try and see if we can navigate our way into glimpsing these apparently removed realities as having something to do with each other after all.

A little note of disclosure: when I talk about Church, my first point of reference is the Church of which I am a member, the Catholic Church, that grouping of baptized Christians whose communion with each other includes, and is in some sense guaranteed by, the successor of Peter. However, by no means does the word "Church" have the same resonances for all of you. So for those of you for whom the word has different associations, please see whether you can find useful analogies between what I say here and your own experience of being able, or unable, to participate in some form of Christian group belonging.

You will probably have heard many different ways of talking about what "the Church" is, many of them quite frightening (in just the same way that many ways of talking about the Bible are frightening). You get the impression that you are hearing a discourse about power, or a discourse emerging from ownership of "position", or a justification and defence of traditional and historical prerogatives. It is not necessarily the clerical caste in the Church who talk in these ways, though we are particularly susceptible to it. Often enough lay people, politicians and others, will also wield "the Church" as a weapon in cultural wars in much the same way as others wield "the Bible". Indeed typically, while the default Protestant error is "bibliolatry" – making an idol of the Bible – the default Catholic error is "ecclesiolatry" – making an idol of the Church. The idol worship to which each of our groups is prone is slightly culturally different, even if the underlying pattern is the same.

When we worship an idol, our love, which is in principle a good thing, is trapped into grasping onto something made in our own image. This "something", which we of course do not perceive as an idol, then becomes the repository for all the security and certainty which we idolaters need in order to survive in the world. We are unaware that the tighter we grasp it, the more insecure and uncertain we in fact become, and the more we empty the object which we idolize of any potential for truth and meaning. And of course because love is in principle a good thing, for us to get untangled from its distorted form is very painful. Nevertheless, against any tendency we might have to blame the idol for being an idol, it is really the pattern of desire in us, the grasping, that is the problem, not the object. For just as the Bible is not an act of communication that we can lay hold of, but the written monuments to an act of communication that takes hold of us, so the Church is not an object that we can grasp, but a sign of our being grasped and held; not something that any of us owns, but the first hints, difficult to perceive, of Another's ownership of us.

In this essay, then, rather than attempting to paint you a picture of the Church as an object, I am going to try something rather more difficult, which is to speak tentatively from within a process of letting go of idolatry. Starting not with some fantasy Church that exists only in textbooks, but assuming that you stand, as I do, within range of the ordinary, humdrum reality of local parishes, sacraments, catechists, liturgies, families, prayers, youth groups, school finance discussions, bishops, papal trips, hospitals, architecture, discussions about the admission and formation of clergy, or about the presence or absence of clergy in your local community.

In addition to these realities, which can vary from the banal to the occasionally heroic, we have experience of a far more dire set of resonances of "Church". The ones most obvious to us currently are those deriving from the great clerical sex-abuse cover-up. But each generation in each part of the world may have some comparable memories: of Vichy bishops giving Hitler salutes, of Argentine bishops backing up torturers, of a Venezuelan hierarch claiming that a series of devastating floods was God's punishment on the people for voting in a way of which he disapproved, of a Romanian patriarch blessing Communist guns, of silver-tongued pastors demonizing oponents and rolling in cash while living double lives, of closeted gay clergy, many with mitres, emotionally blackmailing each other into supporting mendacious attacks on the civil rights of their openly gay brothers and sisters, of rank institutional misogyny and the cheap political use of threatened excommunication.

This is, sadly, by no means an exhaustive list. Nevertheless I take it that these are the kind of things which colour our experience of Church. However, I'm not going to be talking directly about them but instead will be seeking to take further the shifts in relationship, in imagination, in wanting, and in belonging that I've been introducing to you so far in this course. I'm very keen *not* to be trying to tell you to what institutions you must belong in order to be "good". Nor even to try to tell you how I think the visible institutions which we already have should be run or structured, or to offer a critique of them. I take their presence, and their need to be seriously reformed, for granted, but think that what is really important is not what *they* do or say, but how *we* learn to get unhooked, in their midst, and even occasionally with their help, from being run by the "social other" and are empowered instead to be run by the "Other other". In other words, I want to offer you, by means of some images, a way in to a non-idolatrous living of Church, one characterized by a spacious imagination and a complete lack of rivalry in the belonging.

1. The restaurant

No images are entirely reliable as guides to a reality, but I hope you will allow yourself to inhabit each of the images I'm going to propose to you for long enough to see where it might be useful. The first image I'm going to ask you to dwell on, or in, is that of a Really Classy Restaurant. And you are a Really Aristocratic Guest at this Restaurant. You've been invited to it for a magnificent meal, one for which the taste buds even of a Real Aristo like yourself aren't fully prepared, so that the evening will be a learning experience as well as a tasting one.

You have heard of the Chef, though no one has seen him since shortly after the inauguration of the restaurant. It may even be the case, as was suggested by the brilliant detectives from Pixar in their 2007 exposé *Ratatouille*, that the Master Chef is in fact a rat. Certainly the creativity that comes from occupying a place of shame with generosity was beautifully captured in their account of a "repugnant other" as the driving force behind the banquet. In any case, the Chef is busy in the kitchen, behind those swing doors, the sort that waiters can push through while balancing improbable numbers of trays.

You have been invited for two reasons, which are really one: because the Chef likes you, and because he wants to feed you. In fact, this is the Chef's way of showing that he delights in you: by feeding you of his very best in such a way that makes you even more aware of how aristocratic, privileged and fortunate you are. The food is a sign of his delighting in you, and at the same time a nourishment that will put you into a rollicking good humour. Thus it will both enable you to think more imaginatively, and give you the energy to realize whatever it is that your growing good humour suggests that you would really like to accomplish.

Here, as in every classy restaurant, there are waiters and sommeliers whose job it is to scurry back and forth between the kitchen, the cellar and the tables bringing you

menus, suggestions, cutlery, napkins and, eventually, food
and drink to suit you. Except that in this restaurant something is out of synch. The waiters are suffering from a seri-
ous problem of perspective. They seem to think that the
restaurant is all about them, and this of course introduces
an element of farce into the proceedings. I mean, how
many of us go to a restaurant because of the waiters?

Nevertheless, in this restaurant, at the same time as the
Chef is hard at work preparing the food, and the aristocratic guests are beginning to relax into knowing how aristocratic they are at the tables, the waiters, whose task it is to
serve the Chef by serving those whom the Chef wants to
nourish, are engaged in a constant series of drama-queen
hissy fits. Sometimes it is about which one is the Maître
D', or whether there ought to be a Maître D' at all. Then
there are rows about the gender, the marital status, and
(dear Lord!) even the sexual orientation of the waiters.
Then there are endless snits about who has a nicer uniform, who is promoting whose friends, who has been insuf-
ficiently attentive to whose dignity and so forth.
Furthermore, the waiters seem to have picked up, through
their forays into the kitchen, that they are somehow ema-
nations of the Chef, but know better than the Chef who
the guests are, and what is good for them. The result is
that they are inclined to offer the guests very eccentric
accounts of the menu, ones strongly biased towards what
is less effort for themselves. They have a tendency to filter

the very wide list of "specials" into something much narrower, which boosts their own understanding of what the restaurant is about and their place in it. They also come up with strange translations of the menu that make the food sound rather unpalatable.

Sometimes, amidst much rolling of the eyeballs, they make it quite clear that they dislike some of the guests, don't think they should be in the restaurant. They refuse to serve them, or serve them tiny portions, or portions in which they have spat en route to the table. Miraculously they can't actually poison the food. Nevertheless they can so poison the atmosphere as to make even the hardiest guest wonder whether the food isn't poisoned also. Sometimes they withhold bits of cutlery out of spite, while convincing themselves that it's for the guests' own good. All in all, they seem entirely run by their own concerns, driven by what's going on in their own group dynamic. The Chef's guests are, from the waiters' point of view, incidental extras, a backdrop to their own addictive soap opera.

Well, what a show! Just as well that the guests are Really Very Aristocratic. If the guests weren't very aristocratic, they might be inclined to go into rivalry with the waiters, to start protesting, to be dragged into the waiters' internal rows. They might completely lose perspective, and start being sucked into the waiters' delusion that the point of guests being at the restaurant is for the benefit of the waiters. Luckily, as I say, the guests are really Very

Aristocratic, and they know that they have been invited by a Very Aristocratic Chef, the very source of Aristocracy. So, being Aristocratic, they are able to chortle with amusement at the goings-on among the hired help: "Ah well, it's awfully difficult to get good service nowadays!" "Downstairs are playing up again." And rather than being dismayed about the inability of the servants to get their act together, the Aristocratic guests are relaxed about how the Aristocratic Chef is in fact going about the whole thing in an unflummoxed way, and will continuously smuggle delicious food out to the guests, in clever disguises so that the waiters don't notice it, by means of non-uniformed employees whose existence the waiters might well refuse to acknowledge if they could even perceive them.

Isn't it lucky, as I say, that the guests are very aristocratic, so aristocratic in fact that they are not at all sucked into the waiters' soap opera! They can be mildly amused by the goings-on, when they notice them, but not at all obsessive, let alone contemptuous. A real Aristo would never be contemptuous of servants, not being in rivalry with them, but might actually be very fond of them, grateful for their being there at all, tolerant of their foibles, able to see the hilarity of the farce without losing the ability to be pained by its pathos. Having no horse in the race of her servants' rows, a real Aristo might even be able to offer occasional clear-sighted advice to this or that waiter. However, she wouldn't at all let Downstairs' dramas occupy too much of Upstairs' time or attention, which are very properly dedicated to much more enjoyable, creative and leisurely purposes.

Well, I hope the main purpose of the image is clear. I've introduced it in order to facilitate a shift of perspective. Most discussions of what is meant by Church emanate from a waiterly perspective and assume that the Restaurant has much more to do with the waiters than it has. But in fact Church is really all about the Chef making something available for increasingly aristocratic guests, and what the guests then make of the energy they are thereby given. So I'm going to concentrate on these two poles of the image: what's in the kitchen and what it's like to be at the table. We will, eventually, have a brief look at the role of the waiters in all this, but initially I want to get you used to the idea that the waiters (of which I am one) have a proper and genuine role whose perfection in acting out coincides with our near invisibility. Every restaurant has waiters, but no good restaurant is really about the waiters. The very best waiter is the one whose advice, elegance, speed and availability for service enhances your experience of the banquet which the Chef has prepared for you, without ever drawing attention to himself.

2. The halfway house

The next image that I'm going to ask you to inhabit, as we imagine our way through some more shifts of perspective, is that of the Halfway House. In some countries, when people are released from prison after serving long terms, they are not sent straight back to the communities from which they came. Rather, our governments have so disposed it that they spend a period in a halfway house. There they become accustomed to the freedom that is coming upon them, and begin to re-acquire habits of socialization, self-reliance and employability. Habits which they may have had before being sent to prison, but which are likely to have been severely atrophied by their period of institutionalization. Many convicts become so accustomed to prison life that, as their sentences come to an end, they experience considerable fear as to whether they will be able to survive on the outside. A number reoffend very shortly after release in order to be returned to a security which they are unable to provide for themselves. Hence the value of the halfway house: a period of adjustment to freedom, with some supervision, some conditions, some enforced moments of presence, but also some networks, some guidance as to how to cope with a "world out there" which may have altered almost beyond recognition in the fifteen or twenty years since the ex-con was last a regular citizen.

Of course, the very fact that halfway houses exist at all is a sign that those "on the outside" – the authorities and the ordinary citizens of civil society – consider that there are certain normal, decent values, ways of behaving, habits, abilities to care for oneself and one's family, most of which are out of range of those in prison. There are patterns of courtship, mating, procreating and educating, ways to conduct commerce and leisure, all of which are good things in themselves, part of what being a viable free adult is all about. It is because these habits and practices exist so massively "on the outside", however flawed and fragile their living out, that those who are used to them recognize that enforced incarceration in total institutions defined by gender over time has deleterious consequences for personal viability. Long-term imprisonment, more than an extended temporary deprivation of liberty, is an enforced resocialization into a total, but seriously diminished, form of human culture.

It is because those on the outside share among themselves significant elements of an understanding of what is sane and healthy that they know that convicts, who may have had a somewhat weak hold on normal and healthy social habits and practices in the first place, *need help* in being able to move from the diminished and vitiated forms of living together which are cultivated in prison, towards the richer and more open forms which go along with freedom, family, regular employment, creativity and so on.

In other words, however little an ex-con who is coming out of a total institution after, say, twenty years, may understand of what it's going to take for him to be successfully resocialized into the practices and forms of life "on the outside"; however little he may genuinely comprehend quite what a distance he will have to travel before being viable, it is people from those "outside" forms of life who "reach down" as it were, and set up a halfway house, with accompanying social workers, probation officers and employment counsellors, among others, so as to facilitate the draw of the ex-con back into less frightened, more healthy and more productive patterns of getting on with life.

I'd like to explore some ways in which the image of the halfway house can help us reimagine what it is and isn't like living with Church. First some similarities. A central one, perhaps, is that *the Church, like the halfway house, is not an end in itself*. No one thinks that the chief joy of coming out of prison is that you get to go to a halfway house. The halfway house only has existence at all as a staging post, something which has enough elements in common with the sort of life that the prisoner is leaving behind that she not be completely drowned in her own inability to cope with returning to freedom. Nevertheless its whole purpose is to prepare people for freedom, a way of life which has very little in common with what they are used to. This new way of life is one where they will be relied on to be creative, responsible, imaginative, full of initiative, perseverance and so on. In other words, the halfway house exists only as a means at the service of something much greater than itself: forms of social flourishing and togetherness which are initially out of reach of the ex-con. For those who have "come through the system" the idea is that after a time, they become viable in entirely new fields. Then they will have, in the best of cases, only a loose affiliation with the halfway house, an entirely voluntary desire to be associated with it, gratitude for the help derived from their association with it, and a longing to help other ex-cons who are coming through.

Another point of similarity with Church is that the very existence of the halfway house is a firm sign of a benevolent intention implanted by "outside". "Outside" knows what it is like to live well, and knows that those who currently don't know how to do so, owing to their time in prison, are in principle capable of living well and can be nudged beyond their current patterns of desire. The quality of the bricks and mortar of the halfway house, and even the competence of the social workers and probation officers, are secondary to the fact that these are genuine signs, more or less effective signs, of what is a real instantiated project, more or less effectively instantiated, a project which is the fruit of a pattern of desire, a draw, from an outside which knows that there is a way, an arduous way to be sure, of people moving from their prison socialization to their free socialization. *The halfway house, like the Church, is an effective sign of a draw from beyond itself* that is empowering its residents into becoming creators of society.

A third similarity between Church and the halfway house might be that neither is concerned with producing predetermined results. A halfway house is not designed to train ex-cons specifically to be computer programmers, or beauticians, landscape gardeners or air traffic controllers, though any halfway house would be delighted if its former residents were to achieve stable careers in any of those fields. Its purpose is relational, enabling an arduous change in the ex-con's pattern of desire, imagination, capacity for socialization, self-esteem, such that they are no longer constantly liable to trip themselves, and others, up, but are able to imagine some good, one that is in some way matched to the talents and idiosyncrasies that they are coming to discover as their own, a good that they are increasingly equipped to realize as their talents are allowed to develop. The hope is that eventually they be empowered and connected in such a way as to turn renewed imagination into recognizable flourishing. The halfway house is a structured space in which people move beyond merely being free *from* something (enforced confinement) to being free *for* something: constructive and creative involvement with society. Likewise, Church is a structured space in which people move beyond being free from something (being run by death and its fear) to being free for something: constructive and creative involvement in new forms of togetherness and enjoyment.

So: not an end in itself, but an effective sign of a draw from beyond itself, whose hoped-for outcome is free lives run by changed patterns of desire. Well, so far so good. But in fact all of these similarities depend on something which is in evidence when it comes to halfway houses, but not at all in evidence when it comes to Church, and this is the way in which a more or less healthy "outside" society is what people are used to. In our normal countries "outside" is vastly bigger than "inside": those who are in prison are, it is to be hoped, a tiny minority of the populace; they are there because of failures to respect the norms of healthy outside life, and their presence there is a more or less long-term, but in principle, a temporary, abstraction from where they normally belong. Thus, from the point of view of those in prison the existence of a halfway house is a comparatively banal statement of the values of the wider society, an indication of a continuity between life on the outside and life on the inside, along with a helping hand to face the challenges of adapting to a less structured normalcy. None of those inside a prison deny the existence of an "outside", even those who will in fact never see it again. So the fact of the existence of a halfway house is not, in itself a very revolutionary or radical statement.

3. The portal

When it comes to seeing the Church as halfway house, however, something much weirder is going on, something requiring a much greater rupture in our imagination. Because the image starts from the recognition that *everyone* is in prison, and *no one* has ever had a previous regular normal life on the outside. In fact, of ourselves, we would not even know that there was such a thing as life on the outside, let alone that it might be available for us, and that we can be, as it were, retro-fitted for it.

And here of course is what is odd: when everyone is in prison, and always has been, and it is the only reality that everyone knows, then of course it doesn't appear to anyone that they are in prison. What they are is normal, and life just is what it is. Remember how long it took Jim Carrey in *The Truman Show* to learn that there was an "outside" to his "normal" world? It is only when such people receive a communication from someone who is not in prison that they learn that they are in prison. A communication from someone who is entirely outside their social and cultural world: someone who offers signs of being from somewhere else, and of there actually being a somewhere else which is in fact more truly where all those who are in prison are from and for which they are capable of being refitted.

Now please notice the shocking quality of the act of communication: the good news that you needn't be in prison and weren't made for prison inevitably also communicates the beginnings of an awareness that what you regard as normal may more properly be characterized as "being in prison". This awareness, and the new characterization of your situation which comes with it, an awareness which depends entirely on your taking on board a regard from outside, may be perceived as quite intolerable!

Well, this of course is what is central to imagining Church. As humans we were quite literally unable to begin to imagine that there might be such a thing as life not run by death. All of our presuppositions are death-laden ones in ways which we couldn't even recognize as such until something that wasn't part of our culture structured by death unfurled itself in our midst. It was unimaginable that what seemed to us to be simply normal might in fact be a symptom of our having become trapped in something less than ourselves. And yet that is what the entire burden of our "Forgiving Victim" course has been: we are being inducted into becoming able to imagine the deathless One unfurling deathlessness as a human life story in our midst in such a way that we can share it and begin to participate in a deathless sociality as that for which we were really made.

Given this, I hope you can see that whereas an ordinary halfway house is a comparatively banal conduit between two social realities, the unfurling of the beginnings of a deathless sociality and the possibility of our being inducted into it, in the midst of our death-run culture, implies much more of a rupture. A shuttle docking at the International Space Station to take the astronauts who've been spending a few months there back to Earth is experienced by the astronauts as part of a certain continuity. However, a portal from another universe opening itself up over the White House lawn and beginning to communicate with us about taking us into the other universe, asking us to trust that that universe is more fully our home than the one we know, is much more of a shake-up.

Yet this latter picture is the more accurate analogy with Church: a completely unknown social reality has started to instantiate itself in our midst, thus entirely altering our understanding of the social reality which we took for normal. It is one thing to know where you are, and know that there is an elsewhere, and that there is a way to get adapted to life elsewhere. It is quite another when a previously unknown "elsewhere" turns up and is *just there* making elsewhere available to you starting now. Where you are, what you are used to, is now completely and shockingly relativized. So in this way the Church is quite unlike most halfway houses. The very fact of its existence, which is the same as the beginnings of the new form of living together which it contains, is already an irruption of elsewhere. It is a reality-altering statement, or sign, of an unimaginably powerful "just there" alongside, and breaking into, what we had taken for granted as normal.

4. Shifts in perspective

I hope it is by now clear quite how different the same reality can look, depending on where you find yourself as it arrives. Those who share our culture are perfectly at liberty to see it as not a halfway house at all. The portal that has opened up on the lawn does look remarkably like a dead criminal, executed under shameful circumstances. A failure like that scarcely seems like an act of communication, much less an opening into a richer universe that is *just there*, palpitating alongside our own.

For many in our culture the visible elements of the halfway house are merely signs of the strange obsession, or escapism, of some within our culture, pointing to nothing beyond that. The "portal on the lawn" is simply a hologram set up by clever projectors behind the bushes. Such people have no sense of a regard on us all from an "outside" which knows of a healthier form of human flourishing. It is logical, therefore, that they should have no sense of being trapped on the "inside" of something that is an atrophied or distorted form of being.

Nevertheless, even those of us who are beginning to undergo the draw of the act of communication, to sense it for what it is, we too are almost entirely run by the same patterns of desire and imagination as all the rest of our fellow humans, so it takes some time for our perception of what is going on to shift. Indeed, the first impression that someone would get if they perceive a previously unknown "elsewhere" opening up a portal inside their reality, is not: "Oh, someone's setting up a halfway house." The first impression is: "We're being invaded!" Then after a time, as what has happened sinks in, the second impression is: "What looked like an invasion is beginning to look more like a prison break-in, of all absurd things." And it's worth remembering that this is the sort of imagery which Jesus uses in the New Testament – a thief in the night breaking unexpectedly through a wall into a house. I use the image of "prison break-in", because as what's really going on in the "invasion" begins to become clear, it also becomes clear that the "invasion" – an unfriendly term – is in fact an "irruption" – a friendly term – into a reality which seemed normal, but in the light of the irruption is being seen for what it is: a hostile form of existence, a form of prison, an unnecessary confinement.

As time goes on, the perspective shifts again: what looked like a prison break-in has had the effect of producing a gaping hole in the prison fabric, the portal through which "elsewhere" has been unfurled in our midst. So some people, seeing the hole in the fabric of their reality, imagine that "elsewhere" is to be found by going – somewhere else. In other words, that what has been opened up is a form of escape from prison. Not a halfway house, but a hole through which they can climb in order to get somewhere else. For these people there is really no such thing as a halfway house, a process by which they can be drawn into a new socialization. There is simply what they have discovered to be a bad socialization, from which they have been given an exit hatch, without any particular notion of what any good socialization might look like. For such people (and many modern Christians are of this sort), Church may point to a reality "outside", but it doesn't contain within itself the beginnings of the reality to which it is pointing. It is not a portal by which another reality begins to instantiate itself in our midst, but a hole through which we climb into a better place. There is rupture, but no real continuity.

However (and this is where I love the Catholic "thing"), if we stick around with the perception of the prison break-in, and the portal, for long enough, we begin to notice something rather odd: a prison with a hole in it which is just there, and just stays open, isn't really a prison. A prison with a temporary hole in it, a tunnel made by some escaping prisoners, or by friends of theirs from the outside, becomes an effective prison again the moment its authorities seal the escape route. However, any prison in which there emerges an uncloseable hole ceases to be a prison and becomes a quite different sort of collective. While some in it may prefer the stability and order of life before the hole, and act as though there were no hole in the system, the fact is that the entire system has now been altered. It has become not only possible, but normal, to reconceptualize "inside": what used to be a closed system which didn't even know it was closed, turns out instead to be a satellite reality dependent on a huge and massively healthy "outside" whose existence had not previously been suspected.

It is as this perception develops and stabilizes that the image of the "halfway house" comes into its own. The shock of the rupture yields to the realization of the continuing "just there" of the "elsewhere" that is instantiating itself via the portal in our midst. And with it the realization of quite what a small satellite our reality is to the "elsewhere" that is beginning to draw us into its orbit. Eventually, along with this there develops the realization that the portal is habitable, that it is training us to start to be already what we were always meant to be, and didn't know it. So "Church" can begin to be understood as a quite normal function of the "just there" of the portal, a stable sign of a healthy sociality from beyond which is reaching into our midst in quite regular ways to draw us out of our diminished culture of togetherness marked by death and start to make us viable creators of new, deathless, forms of togetherness.

It is here, alas, that Catholics, of whom I am one, become presumptuous. So sure are we, and rightly so, of the "just there" which is unfurling itself in our midst, so clear to us is it that humans are not really prisoners, yet have all been accidentally born in and formed by prison, and are now being empowered to be citizens of elsewhere, that we forget that we are, all of us, still, largely formed from within by the pattern of desire which seemed normal in prison. The result is that we play down the rupture which the portal has introduced into our manner of being together, and assume too easily that the stable, regular objectivity of "just there" is like the stable regular objectivity that we knew from prison. And the result is that we are far too often inattentive to the ways in which we are treating as part of the stability and order of "Elsewhere" things which are in fact part of the oppressive, death-ridden order and fake stability enjoined on us by the prison officers and administrators of the system that is passing away.

The challenge is to be sensitive both to the rupture and the continuity simultaneously – and that is a great challenge. Becoming sensitive to this is part of becoming alive to the sheer vivacity and variety, the sense of fun, the desire for our delight, the essential lack of seriousness by which the Other other is inclined to scandalize our narrow little hearts.

5. The embassy

One further shift in perception tied to my inadequate, ever-shifting, "halfway house" model of the Church. After a bit, what seems like a halfway house morphs into an embassy. The image is easy to understand. An embassy is a portal of another country in the midst of our own. We recognize that once a person is through the gates of a country's embassy, then they are on the sovereign soil of that country, even though the embassy building be physically located in the midst of one of our cities. That person cannot be hauled out by our own armed forces, as they could be if they were, for instance, a bank robber who had "gone to ground" in a warehouse. Furthermore, the employees of the embassy are typically citizens of the country whose embassy it is, and they come among the citizens of our country as the bearers of the values and the interests of their own country. They sign to us by their presence that "elsewhere" is not only geographically removed, but is also in our midst; when they look at us we are being gazed at, from close up, with a regard formed by "elsewhere". And their gaze, if we are drawn to it, can teach us to look at our own country and values in a quite different light from the ones to which we are accustomed. Their boss is the Ambassador, but they are all ambassadors in the sense that each one, by being who they are, instantiates the Embassy.

We also use the word "ambassador" in a looser sense. People who have gone through a particular course of training, and become particularly fine examples of what this school, or that apprenticeship, hopes to turn out, are then treated as "ambassadors" – bearers before the public of the values for which the institution in question would like to be recognized. You can imagine, then, that some, indeed hopefully all, of the residents of a halfway house will eventually be able to be regarded as its "ambassadors" – people who can be seen as its success stories. Not ex-cons who were merely grudgingly reinserted into "outside" values, but people who have become shining examples of what those outside values are about, and are unashamed of it being known that it was the help they received through the halfway house that equipped them, say, to set up and run a small business, itself employing various other ex-cons.

Well, the oddity of Church is that it is not only the sign of a prison break-in that creates a rupture in the fabric of the system, opening us up to an outside that is "just there"; it is not only an escape tunnel to get outside the system; it is not even only a halfway house, by which ex-cons can be stably and regularly drawn into the forms of socialization which are proper to life on the outside, but it is a portal of "just there" solidly implanted in the territory of here which turns ex-cons round completely. They come to find their real citizenship in the country that is "just there", and take on board its values in such a way that they are transformed into ambassadors of another kingdom and what it's about. In other words, the whole point of the portal is not to extract people from prison and send them somewhere else, but to "turn" apparent citizens of one reality into active agents of another. This happens when these people discover their real citizenship in another reality and take that citizenship on board so completely that they can become part of the irruption, the breaking in, the effective instantiation in our midst, of the deathless life that the portal has opened up.

In Essay 6, when we looked at the Fernando story, we saw how Paul talks about the role of being "ambassador for Christ", and I suggested that this meant someone who has allowed themselves to be forgiven by the class fairy who is not run by the space of shame, and so has themselves become an imitator of the class fairy, being themselves prepared to occupy the space of shame, fear and death without being run by it. I hope you can see now how this Embassy might work: part of the work of the portal, its halfway house function, is to enable us to get used not to being run by death, shame, fear and rivalry until such a time as we find ourselves "turned" so that we can actually become part of its Embassy function.

But please notice what this "turning" does to my inadequate "halfway house" image: it deprives it of an "elsewhere", a healthy outside society, for which ex-cons are being prepared, so that they can leave behind prison life for ever. It turns out that the portal that has opened up has never had any intention of taking any of us "elsewhere", which would suggest a certain despair about, or contempt for, the reality into which the portal has inserted itself. On the contrary. It turns out that the only "elsewhere" is *here*, beginning to be instantiated in our midst by signs that contain and produce the reality that they are pointing to. The result is that the Embassy-creating portal is turning the reality which we have perceived as prison "on our way out of it" into the adventure playground that it was always meant to be. It is not so much taking our reality by *storm* – a military image suggesting one reality which takes over another and shuts it down – as taking it by *surprise*, so that it begins to yield delighted glimpses and gasps of of what is coming into it, and what it is becoming.

6. Rules and officers

Well, I hope that it is more or less obvious that what I have been trying to do with you is get across something of the notion of "sacramentality": insinuations of how the irruption of the Other other in our midst has a regular shape that we call Church. I want to ask you to notice a couple of things derived from the shifting perspective that I've been trying to illustrate for you. And this is how very different "rules" and "clerical leadership" look if we consider them according to my "morphing halfway house" model of Church. I mention these two, since they are both issues which can become unhealthy fixations (whether of love or of hatred) and my whole purpose here is to facilitate freedom from idolatry.

The only difference initially as regards pattern of desire between those who are in prison but don't know it, and those who are being persuaded of the portal's invitation and are just beginning to move into a halfway house, is that the latter, having received hints of a regard from outside, have some sense that their imagination and pattern of desire is atrophied and distorted. But this scarcely makes them any more capable of imagining and desiring healthy forms of living.

For at least his first few days in a halfway house, and even though his heart be singing at what is opening up for him, the ex-con is hardly any less atrophied and distorted in his desire, expectations, and ways of relating than his former cell mates who have remained in prison. What is also odd is that from the point of view of his former cell mates, those who are in prison but don't know it since for them there is no outside, the halfway house does not at all look like what it claims to be – a staging post en route to a yet to be imagined freedom. Quite the reverse. It looks like a series of restrictions on such freedoms as they already have, and pointless and arbitrary restrictions at that.

Let's explore this gap in perception by means of an example. You can imagine that it might be a normal part of life in a particular culture to tell lies for immediate gain. Those within that culture know this, understand it, are used to this, and participate in it. The result is that people don't really believe each other, consistently treat each other, and thus themselves, as means, not ends, and consequently are not prepared to entrust each other with much. Overall the group is pretty stagnant: consider how weak and unstable commerce, for instance, would be in such a culture. Now imagine that there is another culture where truthfulness is the norm, and because truthfulness is the norm, people can entrust things, roles, projects, deals, to each other, and all move ahead very well because of the cooperation this engenders. For these latter people, the instruction "Don't tell lies" is redundant, moot, since truthfulness is habitual to them, and they already enjoy all the benefits that come from living in this way.

However, for a denizen of the "lying is normal" world, it

is not at all clear that there is such a thing as a world of habitual truthfulness, nor can they imagine any benefits to be had from it. So if it were the case that the inhabitants of the habitually truthful world were to set up a halfway house to enable habitual liars to be drawn into their world, the halfway house would look, from the perspective of those outside it, and even from the perspective of those recently inside it, like a pretty restrictive place. It would appear to them under the sign of a prohibition: "Thou shalt not tell lies." For dwellers in the "lying is normal" world, this would simply be a silly, and purely negative, interference with their normal way of doing things. Even for many of those recently entering the halfway house, they would have to trust the good intentions of those who had set it up, for initially there would be no profit for them in obeying the prohibition, merely the inconvenience. For the only way to taste the value of habitual truthfulness is by being habitually truthful.

Until such a time as you are habitually truthful, then, you may find yourself having painfully, and on an incident by incident basis, to forego the immediate gains you are accustomed to getting from lies, without seeing any positive return. Only when it doesn't occur to you to reach for the immediate gains will you start to see that you have already been receiving a whole lot of non-immediate gains in terms of how other people treat you, how you are able to treat them, and what you are able to do together. These gains were entirely invisible to you before, and are so obvious to you now as not even to seem gains, but normality, just part of what being human is all about. From your new habitually truthful persona it is perfectly clear that the culture of habitual lies is not even really a human culture in its own right, simply a terribly atrophied and distorted version of what it might be but can't imagine. Part of its distortion is that of being locked into rivalry with the absolute prohibition "Do not tell lies." This has the effect that from within the culture of habitual lies, the culture of habitual truthfulness cannot be seen for what it is, but appears as a restrictive culture absolutely centred on a prohibition.

I stress this, since one of the joys of life within the Church is actually discovering that prohibitions have no real place in it at all. They are merely the moot remnants of what things looked like before you found yourself sucked into a new way of life. Once you are living it, on the inside of it, you gradually lose your need for a description of what it looks like to trespass outside it, since you are becoming free even of being able to imagine trespassing. All your freedom is *for*, to such an extent that you don't really understand any more what freedom *from* is from: you are so entirely dedicated to what is constructively appropriate that all prohibitions are moot.[12]

---

[12] Cf. 1 Corinthians 6.12 where St Paul says "'All things are lawful for me' – but not all things are beneficial – 'All things are lawful for me' – but I will not be dominated by anything."

So life in this halfway house really does look completely different depending on the perspective of different patterns of desire and imagination. For some people, it is simply a derangement, for others a place of cruel and pointless restrictions. Even for those coming close to it, at first its narrowness and sobriety is quite frightening, for they are having to trust what is not evident: that there is a world of freedom beyond the restrictions, that the restrictions are only the entry point into a process of rehabituation. For the moment they will have to trust the probation officers, psychologists and employment counsellors to help them find their way into enjoying that rehabituation from within. Sometimes, initially, what they now recognize to be the prison they have left behind will seem to be positively attractive by comparison.

Well, this brings up the thorny issue of the officers! In most halfway houses, comparatively few of the probation officers, psychologists and employment counsellors are themselves ex-cons (though some may be, and it is difficult to think of a better training). They are people from the outside who are employed by others on the outside in order to facilitate the acclimatization of the ex-cons into their new outside reality. They are, if you like, already visibly and imitably competent fully habituated citizens of the healthy social reality. Their job is to be part of the draw which makes the halfway house a sign of something beyond itself.

However, in the halfway house that is the Church there

is not a single officer who is not just as much an ex-con as all the other residents. Every one of us started in prison, like everybody else; and our imaginations and patterns of desire, despite, and sometimes because of, our intensive training and style of life, are just as subject to lapsing back into the habitual cultural patterns of prison life.

If a prisoner who doesn't realize she's in prison is confronted with someone who claims to be a probation officer mandated by a social reality of whose existence she, the prisoner, is ignorant, she doesn't see a probation officer from elsewhere, she sees just another representative of "law and order" – a prison guard with a gaudily coloured uniform. That's no surprise. However it is also the case that all of us who are more or less newly arrived residents in the halfway house also find it difficult at first to distinguish between those whom we now understand to have been prison guards, to dealing with whom we are used, and probation officers, who at first seem awfully like prison guards. Only with great difficulty do we come to perceive that there are social workers and psychologists whose joy it is to help us get adjusted to a new reality, and that this is not the same as the similarly uniformed people who brainwashed and sedated us in prison in order to make us more functional and manageable. And it is even more difficult for us to reach the stage where we perceive from any of the counsellors hints of direction for future employment in the new society, rather than barks that we should stop dreaming and instead get useful in maintaining the prison economy.

And of course, the officers themselves, since they are also ex-cons in different stages of resocialization, are as likely to have difficulties of perception in this field as everyone else, or more likely. Think of it like this: after a comparatively short time in a halfway house, you are told that you are to be a probation officer, or an employment counsellor. But you have either no experience at all, or merely the tiniest hint of an intuition, of what the healthy society you are supposed to be inducting people into is like, and your only experience of uniformed officials is prison guards. Well, it is scarcely surprising that you will, at least initially, be much more like a prison guard than like a probation officer, much more inclined to react to a changing situation by calling for lockdown than by helping the residents imagine creative new possibilities for the freedom that is coming upon them. And of course, there will be plenty of halfway house residents who will be glad that you are like a prison guard – it enables you to be part of a give and take with which they are familiar, and so helps them put off the arduous training of imagination and desire which will equip you and them to be socialized into the new society.

7. The Banquet

At this point I would like to reintroduce, but in a slightly different form, the image with which we started, that of

the aristocratic guests in the restaurant. That image, morphing now into an image of a Banquet, takes us into the
full reality of the draw and power emanating from the
"healthy outside society". For this healthy outside society is
a party which has gate-crashed into what turns out to be
our prison, set up a portal from elsewhere which is "just
there", opened up a halfway house to enable us to be resocialized, and started to staff an embasssy so that signs of
"just there" begin to transform from within our perception
of "here". Just beneath the surface of each of these images
and palpitating at the centre of all of them, is the image of
a Banquet, actually a Wedding Banquet. This banquet has
already begun, and the consummation which it is celebrat-
ing is already taking place. Yet it unfurls itself amongst us
as something already now reaching into our midst from a
future we cannot grasp, something which is beginning to
turn us into signs of a becoming in which we are held
securely. This is, of course, the central reality which is
made available to us through the Mass.

One of the things which gets very little attention when
people discuss the heavenly banquet, the marriage supper
of the lamb, is the nature of the joy involved. And when
people talk about heavenly joy, you sometimes get the
impression that they are talking about something rather
linear, and pure and rarified. I wonder whether this is really bearable. If a party is for us, then it is for us to enjoy at
least *starting* with our sense of humour, and because the

host actually really likes *us* and wants *our* company. Indeed, likes our company so much that, of all ludicrous things, he wants to *marry us*, take us into sharing his life on terms of equality! So I would like to suggest that we allow a certain raucousness of humour, spilling over from the banquet, to break through to us.

We are all aware that laughter and humour can be very cruel, and cruel laughter would scarcely be compatible with the joy emanating from the banquet. There is however a form of laughter and humour which is entirely without cruelty, which is in fact one of the firmest signs that there could be of the absence of cruelty, and of the presence of general health and sane enjoyment; and that is when people are able to laugh *at themselves*. We've perhaps all been in a situation where someone has started to laugh at us, in a way which might have seemed ironic, for we were indeed doing something ridiculous, but as they laugh we find ourselves noticing that their laughter is not out to get us, it is for us, enjoys us and welcomes us in. Rather than becoming all defensive, grim, and closed down, we find that their laughter lightens us up, so that we are able to receive ourselves again through their perception of us. Thus we can let go of our brittleness, our defensiveness, are enabled to climb down from whatever postures of pretentiousness we were grasping on to and find that we are able to join in with all the mucky-seeming others who are going through the same thing in a growing cacophony of shared delight. It's as we go through this process of laughing at ourselves along with others that we discover how like them we are, what fun it is to be with them, and how much fun it is going to be to enjoy them more in the future.

Earlier, when we were looking at the image of the aristocratic guests at the meal, I asked you to consider something of the mixture of hilarity and pathos which enables these guests to put up with the more or less farcical behaviour of the waiters, and now I would like to see if we can inhabit the tension between that hilarity and that pathos a little more fully. For it is easy enough to see that the waiters, who have now morphed into scarcely prepared probation officers in the halfway house, are run by patterns of behaviour so contrary to that of which we are supposed to be becoming signs, that the guests are simply scandalized by us, go into indignation at us – and Lord alone knows we have given grounds for this indignation.

The tension which holds together the hilarity and the pathos, allowing each to be filled out by the other without being collapsed, is, I think, one of the most difficult things to gesture towards successfully. How can you talk about a dynamic which enables you simultaneously to treat something extremely seriously, and yet not take it seriously at all? The tension hints at something of the power of the passion for us, the inside taste of the love for us, that shapes our host's besottedness. A power which begins to be sensed in our midst as the ability to laugh at ourselves as we find ourselves being forgiven, becoming self-critical, brought into a new way of enjoying togetherness; and yet a power that has a longing for us, a concern for our well-being so strong that we are tempted to use words like "anger" to describe its pathos at our constant and persistent rejection of its invitations. I wonder whether exactly the same longing, love and joy which is experienced by us as an ability not to take ourselves seriously and to laugh at ourselves as we are "let off" our pretentiousness and become self-critical, is not also experienced as wrath by those whose sense of righteousness clings to an impossibility of being tickled by ridicule. And curiously, the richness and joy of finding ourselves able to laugh at ourselves, is not diminished, but enhanced, by the fact that it constantly stretches us out with pathos towards those who most seem averse to it. Which means also the bits of ourselves that seem most averse to it. In other words, part of the joy of the hilarity that is coming upon us is precisely its gentle, stretched refusal to concede definite existence to a "they" off whom our laughter might cruelly rebound, condemned to a separate sphere of ever more fixated seriousness.

I bring this out here since I think that being able to inhabit this tension between hilarity and pathos, tickled by the hidden bursts of mirth that are summoning us into the banquet, is an essential element of life in the Church. It is this tension which empowers us not to be in rivalry with each other, not to be indignant with each other, to with-stand the siren lure of being scandalized by each other, and I suspect that this tension is going to be vital if we are to give flesh to God's project.

Think, for instance of these words, emanating out from the Banquet. Their speaker seems to know so well how we are inclined to collapse the tension into either cruel laughter or cruel righteousness. I suspect that these words, words which last for ever, were not given to us as "critical snark" designed to make us look at each other in a jaundiced and cynical way. I suspect that it is because the Presence who opens up the portal knows how difficult it is for us not to hurt each other that he gives us these words. They are there to protect us from each other as we grow out of prison thought. They remind us how much bigger and more spacious is the project that is seeking to make us free than our frightened, prison-run imaginations will allow.

Consider this:

> *"You know that the rulers of the Gentiles lord it over them, and their great ones exercise authority over them. Not so shall it be among you: but whosoever would become great among you shall be your servant; and whosoever would be first among you shall be your slave: even as the Son of man came not to be served, but to serve, and to give his life as a ransom for many."* [13]

---

[13] Matthew 20.25b–28.

So the titles, the costumes, the weightiness of tone, the gravity of attitude, are pure kitsch, fading remnants of prison life, unless they are brought to life by someone who is throwing themselves lightly into being your servant, which means finding out and ministering to your actual needs, not to what they tell you your needs should be. Only those who are prepared to sit lightly to being a nobody will be found, to their own surprise, to have become a somebody!

Or this:

> "How can you believe, who receive glory from one another and do not seek the glory that comes from the only God?"[14]

Are we, or our officers, locked into dependence on each other's approval, which is part of prison life, rather than acting as sons and daughters whose approval comes from elsewhere, acting from beyond being frightened, blackmailed and ashamed?

Or this:

> "Beware the leaven of the Pharisees, which is hypocrisy. Nothing is covered up that will not be revealed, or hidden that will not be known."[15]

So we are encouraged to learn to be *systemically* self-critical – it's not just this or that bad apple that covers up. Fake goodness imposes itself as a system, a leaven, which runs people, starting with ourselves, and we must always be on the watch for it.

---

[14] John 5.44.
[15] Luke 12.1b–2.

Or this:

> "You ... make void the word of God through your
> tradition which you hand on." [16]

So there is a real difference, and one to which we are
encouraged to be ever attentive, between the apparent
incorrigibility of our ideological systems of goodness and
the unchanging "just there" which is a living, delighting, act
of communication producing huge and constant changes in
our ways of understanding each other and living together;

Or this:

> "They bind heavy burdens, hard to bear, and lay
> them on men's shoulders; but they themselves will
> not lift a finger to move them." [17]

"The system suits us, adjust yourself to it if you want to
belong on our terms, which are the only real terms."

Or this:

> "You blind guides, you strain out gnats and
> swallow camels." [18]

This might translate as "We strain out condoms and
swallow wars" – please be encouraged to continue self-crit-
ically in this vein!

Or this:

> "But you are not to be called rabbi, for you have
> one teacher, and you are all brethren ... you have
> one master, the Christ." [19]

---

[16] Mark 7.13.
[17] Matthew 23.4.
[18] Matthew 23.24.
[19] Matthew 23.8, 10b.

The one master, the dynamo of Presence in the portal, is always *just there*, his teaching and example always alive independently of any of us. So anyone who would teach in Christ's name is always to us as one on the same level as us, as one whose job it is to enliven among us the sign that the Master is producing. Someone who insists on their authority will always be an anti-sign, and we will be right to suspect them. Where true authority has been given it will always be sensed in the enlivening of the sign in those being taught, and in the transparency and loss of self-importance of the one teaching.

What I find curious, and what we officers or waiters find hard to take from these words of Jesus, and many others like them, is this. Precisely because the portal which has opened up for us all is much more of a rupture than a continuity; and precisely because all of us, officers included, have a very slow, arduous path out of having our minds and hearts run by the patterns of prison; so the very same Presence who gifts us with signs of himself as Priest and Teacher, turning particular ex-cons into probation officers, counsellors and the like, this same Presence simultaneously gifts us with a *strongly quizzical* presumption concerning the officer being out of synch with what he's supposed to be about, and does so as part of the education of all of us in freedom.

All the phrases that I have quoted above tend to encourage in us, as a normal part of growth in health in the new

Kingdom, an instinctive suspicion of religious leaders, a presumption of pretension until the contrary is demonstrated. They suggest that we are right always to ask, with relation to any religious teaching "*Cui bono*?" Whom does it benefit? If it is really from God then it is for our benefit. Our benefit is the criterion of its Godliness. Maybe it will take time for us to understand why it is beneficial, because the freedom that is coming upon us is so difficult for us to imagine; but there is also the real possibility that such and such a teaching is just one of those things that may have seemed, and even been, helpful at one time, but is now being shown up as part of the prison structure of fake goodness which we should learn to leave behind. The active and creative ability to discern in this area is an intrinsic part of the gift of life in the halfway house as it morphs into the banquet.[20]

I hope you can see how this ties in with the image of the Restaurant with which we started. The Really Aristocratic guests do not despise their waiters, even as their relationship to them is undergirded with a giggle. The guests are aware of quite what a curious task the waiters have been given in appearing to face them from the same "side" as the Chef. All of us undergo an arduous transformation of imagination and desire in our passage from the prison, through the halfway house, into becoming well-equipped

---

[20] Cf. 1 Thessalonians 5.19–22: "Do not quench the Spirit. Do not despise prophetic words; rather test everything, hold fast to what is good; abstain from every form of evil."

ambassadors of the Portal. But not all of us are commissioned to be signs of the Portal's draw to those alongside us within the halfway house, signs made alive as those commissioned and those with whom they interact blossom publicly into lives shaped as purification from fake goodness. If the Priestly vocation is to undertake the route from "magnificently decked-out offerer of sacrifice" to "visibly generous dweller in the victimary space of shame", then it is fair to say that the life story thrown up by a faithful traversing of that route will not lend itself to obvious charting. If the Preacher's vocation is "Be a professional hypocrite who will become an authentic sign of Christ in your publicly being set free from your own hypocrisy as a truthfulness not your own comes upon you", then it is fair to say that the calling does not come with a straightforward career path.

Conclusion

Well, I apologize for this barrage of images. I have wanted to offer some ways in to a less idolatrous living out of the reality of "Church". Every one of us is liable to be sifted by the shocking realization of how easy it is to become the enablers of a self-serving rhetoric which passes as "good" and "holy" and yet is entirely run by the pattern of desire that is proper to prison, tending towards lockdown; how easy it is to be fully committed to thinking we are acting as supervisors or educators from the Halfway House, or even the Embassy, while in fact we are the pig of prison administration, gaudily decked out with lipstick borrowed from "Elsewhere". And every one of us is right, as part of our process of growing in life in the halfway house, to be learning to discern, gently, aristocratically whether those who claim they are "serving" us or "teaching" us are in fact doing any such thing. It is part of our increasingly relaxed, non-rivalrous way of being in the Halfway House that we be regularly quizzical as to whether it is in fact the One Master who is speaking himself into being in us through this or that official, this or that pronouncement. Maybe it is rather the case that, even as the Master tries to nudge the officials (people like us, and alongside us, whom he really rather likes) beyond cowardice tricked out as obedience, at the same time his love, service and teaching, his hilarity and the pathos which deepens it, is spilling past those officials to reach us through conduits whose freedom from self-importance are a better match for the message.

ESSAY ELEVEN

A little family upheaval

Introduction

You may remember how, at the very beginning of our course, we looked at this passage from the Epistle to the Hebrews.[21]

In many and various ways God spoke of old to our fathers by the prophets; but in these last days he has spoken to us by a Son, whom he appointed the heir of all things, through whom also he created the world.

The passage seemed to start out by talking in a way which, whether we believed it or not, was at least a more or less recognizable form of discourse. However, pretty quickly the author of the passage "jumped the shark", by telling us that the historical person to whom he is referring, Jesus, was somehow involved in the creation of the world. That everything had in fact been made through him. I compared this to a "Napoleon" moment: an apparently

---

[21] Hebrews 1.1–2.

rational interlocutor suddenly slips into the conversation the matter-of-fact observation that he is in fact Napoleon, and then carries on unembarrassed, as though no normal listener would be fazed by the revelation that they are being addressed by L'Empereur himself.

Well, now, as we near the end of the course, we are in a better position to make some sense of that apparent "Napoleon" moment. And like all true crazies, rather than blushing and backing down from my little slip, I'm going to double down on it. Because it's not just an incidental "extra" in the New Testament, which turns up in one or two fringe texts. It turns up explicitly in several places,[22] and implicitly, which means narratively, it turns up, as I will show you, right in the centre of everything. The vision that yields that "Napoleon" moment is central to the whole explosion of meaning which has thrown up the New Testament as its monument. I rather hope that during our course we've undergone enough shifts in our understanding that now we will be able to find ourselves on the inside of this vision without too much difficulty!

Let me just remind you briefly of one of those shifts to prepare us for the delicacy of what I hope to introduce you to. You may remember that, when we looked at the Burning Bush passage in Essay 4 I tried to bring out the

---

[22] John 1.1–2; 1 Corinthians 8.6; Colossians 1.15–20; Ephesians 1.3–14. You might find it interesting to look up some of these texts for yourself, to see if they make more sense after what you have been exposed to in the following pages!

difference between an "I AM" and a "He, She or It is" account of God. A god who can be referred to as "He, She or It" very quickly becomes a function of our manipulation, an object about whom we can talk, or which we can describe. In doing so, we become the starting place, and the god in question fits in with our scheme of things, making us effectively the real "gods" in the story. With "I AM", on the other hand, the starting place is not us, cannot be grasped by us, and we discover ourselves to be peripheral beings as "I AM" approaches us. In this latter account, the more time we spend in the presence of "I AM", the more we are aware that not only we ourselves, but everything that is, is shot through with what I might call "secondariness": we catch a glimpse of ourselves as real, contingent, alive; we catch ourselves reflecting back that we are held in being by something prior to us, something that is not at the same level as ourselves at all, not in rivalry with anything. This "secondariness" is not a form of diminishment, or being put down, but an accurate and objective sense of createdness, something which can in fact be relaxed into with gratitude.

1. Exploring "secondariness"

In order to have a better sense of this "secondariness", I'm going to ask you to spend a little more time inside the shift I've been setting out. I'm going to ask you to recall a couple of illustrations from earlier in our course. In Essay

6 I asked you to engage in the imaginative exercise of remembering a moment in your past in which you had been forgiven for something. To help kick-start the exercise, I gave as an example little Johnny who had stolen a Mars bar from Mrs O'Reilly's corner store. I asked what it was like for little Johnny to be brought back to the store and to be approached by Mrs O'Reilly. She was not so much forgiving him, as had not been offended by him in the first place: the loss of the Mars bar from her stock had scarcely registered with her as somehow an attack on her. So interested was she in little Johnny's well-being that she had interpreted his having stolen the Mars bar as a sign that there was something wrong with him, and more than anything else, she wanted to make sure that he was OK.

For Johnny, the experience of being forgiven – and for him it was indeed being forgiven, since he knew perfectly well that he'd done something wrong, and was expecting punishment – felt at first like a disorienting challenge. He finds himself held in eyes that are looking at him from a completely unexpected perspective: eyes that are not part of any tit for tat, any system of control, or payback, or desert. And yet, as he allows himself to be looked at by them, as he consents to their gaze, he finds himself being let go from his own guilty weddedness to what he'd done, and taken into the space of a new friendship with Mrs O'Reilly, a new space in which he'd actually become someone he didn't yet know, part of a new "we" into which he was being invited.

The second illustration came in Essay 10, as part of my attempt to bring out the raucous, laughter-filled nature of the joy which is central to the heavenly banquet. I asked you to consider a form of laughter which is not cruel: the laughter which flows when someone is enabled to laugh at themselves. Like an experience of being forgiven, a healthy learning to laugh at yourself is a very delicate and rich experience. It involves learning to detect the laughing eyes of, say, a group of people you are with, as affectionate, not hostile, and not out to get you. So if you laugh along with them, you are not simply agreeing to be "put in your place", consenting to a cruel act of putting you down. Your laughing at yourself is not a subtle form of colluding with the gang of those who are against you, agreeing to your own lynching, as it were. On the contrary, you're able to intuit that the laughter in the eyes of the others is well intentioned, likes you, rejoices in you, doesn't take you too seriously in some areas where maybe you've been tempted to take yourself too seriously. Precisely because those merrily laughing eyes are looking at you with this affection, you find yourself able to accept their invitation to join in with their appreciation of you, to allow them to guide you in how you perceive yourself, to sit loose to whatever bits of self-importance were clouding your ability to join in with them. In fact you are given the gift of being able to receive yourself back graciously and flexibly as part of a richer belonging with them. Far from your being put down by this experience, your having been loosened up has opened you to discovering how much more you are than you had thought, and how much more fun it is to be you with these other people than you had previously imagined.

Well, I hope that it is clear what these experiences have in common. Both little Johnny and the person learning to laugh at themselves started with some sort of sense of self, which they more or less knew about and more or less held to. However, they found themselves undergoing a hugely healthy shift in perception such that *who they are doesn't start with them*. Each of them starts to receive themselves from what is other than themselves, freely, and in a way which opens them out. And furthermore, each of them comes to perceive that this receiving of themselves through the eyes of others is something objective, real, and to be grateful for. Exactly because they are receiving themselves through the eyes of what is other than themselves, they glimpse that their own knowing, their own perceiving, formed as it is by that experience of receiving, is peripheral, is a symptom of something which doesn't start with them. In other words, there is a certain dependence – that "secondariness" I mentioned earlier, if you like – which corresponds to who they are, to their place in the world, to their way of learning about people and things. This secondariness does not go along with any sense of being "second-rate" or "only second". Rather it is accompanied by a sense of relief, and of a possibility of opening out. They will be finding themselves becoming more than they had thought. Elements of their past which had seemed central and sources of fixity, if not fixation, are being relativized, and other elements of their past which had not seemed to be of importance or worth are gradually turning into having been, all along, unexplored, rich foundations for a direction, an achievement and a shared flourishing that is only now beginning to open up.

Let's hold these experiences of "secondariness" a moment longer, if we can, rather than rush through them and on to the next thing. Let's imagine that little Johnny spends time undergoing Mrs O'Reilly's generous move towards him, or that I spend time relishing the way in which my friends are giving me back to myself by drawing me into their laughter at me in such a way that it enables me to laugh at myself. While I'm held in that experience, part of the aliveness of the moment in which I glimpse my "secondariness" is that it is a moment of someone else's presence towards me which opens up for me my own relationship, simultaneously, to my past and to my future. The longer I'm held in their regard, the more easily I am able both to remember, to cope with, my past, and to imagine a future to which I can aspire.

While I am just trudging along by myself, not catching myself in the regard of someone else, it was quite simple: my past is behind me, and there's nothing I can do about it. And my future is before me, and who knows what possible knocks or joys it will bring, other than the usual: death and taxes. However the experience of undergoing something in the present at the hands of someone much stronger than oneself gives us something very curious – a sense, starting strictly in the present, which is the only moment at which I can be reached, that there is an outside to my past and to my future. On the one hand, my "becoming" is enlivened such that I experience being reached from a future that is not yet me but that is pulling me in; and on the other hand, in ways I hadn't anticipated, my past is alive and flexible. Parts of it that seemed important were in fact heading nowhere, and surprising parts of it were already tending, in a friendly way, to the person whom I am now discovering myself to be. Who I thought I was, and who I think I am becoming, are both simultaneously altered by the quality of presence of the other who has moved alongside me – Mrs O'Reilly on the one hand, or my group of raucous friends on the other.

2. An extra-planetary interlude

To take this further, before exploring with you what's going on inside some New Testament narratives, I'm going to ask you to engage in a further imaginative exercise. Please imagine that you are a large, complacent, bureaucratic ruler on a small, firm planet somewhere in space, rather like one of those illustrations from *The Little Prince*. You are convinced that you are standing on stable ground, and appear to have good reason to think so. Things seem pretty regular. You govern all that you survey, dispensing order with what seems to you to be fairness, punishing the bad, and rewarding those who support you in keeping the good, good. You are able to deduce from everything you can see a considerable amount about how things work and how they should be, and in line with that knowledge you have made yourself, to your considerable satisfaction, the master of it all.

Now imagine that in the far horizon of outer space there appears a small dot. Not very important really. However, this dot seems to grow, and grow, and grow. What was in the first place scarcely even an object of curiosity for you and your astronomers turns into something rather bigger. As it gets more and more huge, so does it impinge upon, and then gradually fill out, your field of vision. But in fact, the object is not growing: it is vastly bigger than your planet, an unimaginably large star that appears to be moving towards you at scarcely calculable speed. It seems to be moving out of nowhere, coming ever closer to your planet.

However, that is not in fact, what is going on at all. It is not it that has been moving towards *you*. On the contrary *you* have been gradually pulled in to moving towards *it*. So big is it that its own movement is scarcely detectable, despite that fact that you are being drawn in by its gravitational pull. As you come closer to this star, its own gravita-

tional forces adjust your planet to its orbit. And this caus-
es the axis of your planet to tip, ever so slightly, completely throwing what had seemed like its stability and security.
Now all the dwellers on the planet begin to move in ways
that, from your complacent, bureaucratic standpoint, are
unexpected and unpredictable.

As your planet starts to undergo this new draw, finding
itself in the train of a new direction, you, and of course
your "grateful" subjects, begin to realize, as you look back
at where you had been, that what had, up until now,
seemed so stable and regular, so firm and predictable, was
in fact no such thing. Up until the time when you started
being drawn in to the orbit of the huge star, and way, way
before you began to appreciate that that was what was
going on, the whole of your planet had been dangerously
out of kilter. In a manner far beyond anything which your
planet-bound, complacent, bureaucratic, powers might be
able to control, your planet had been gradually tipping
backwards into the maw of a black hole. This you can only
begin to appreciate now as you find yourself safely in the
draw of the huge star, and can look behind you to see what
had really been going on; and this is something which none
of you, except for a few crazies whose opinions you had
rubbished and whom you had kept out of circulation, had
even begun to be able to perceive before.

As the draw of the huge star pulls the little planet further into its train, a new kind of regularity begins to

emerge in your way of life, a regularity wholly dependent on a star of whose existence you had until recently been entirely ignorant. Imagine your shock, stable and complacent as you are, as you come to perceive how all the stability, all the order over which you thought you had been presiding, had in fact been so much fakery. Real stability and security looks like nothing less than a wild ride adventure of being drawn into the tail of this hugely powerful star. Neither you nor anybody who mattered on your planet had even begun to come close to perceiving what had really been running your show before, when fixity seemed all and movement seemed so threatening. The power of the black hole had been entirely invisible even as it had been sucking you in.

So, the shock, yes, especially for you, since you were so invested in the stability and the order, in what had until just recently passed as goodness. But also the excitement, especially for those under you, many of whom had been burdened by your pretentious righteousness. You can imagine them, rather to your discomfort, beginning to rejoice as they discover parameters of existence and of ways of being, about which your rule had known nothing, and of which it would have heartily disapproved if it had. While you are in shock, they are adjusting remarkably quickly to the delight of finding themselves an unfinished project being drawn into the movement of the immensely powerful star, learning the ropes of who they are to become. You, on the other hand are more or less paralysed, not sure whether to try to batten down the hatches, proclaim that nothing has changed, and reassert your control, or whether in some way, and preferably without being too greatly humiliated, to get with the new direction of things, lower your pretensions and agree to allow yourself to join those whom you thought of as your subjects in being redefined by the unexpected star.

Well, I've given you this image for two reasons. In the first place, it illustrates the change of perspective which occurs when what seemed like a not particularly significant object in your ken moving towards you, turns out to be in fact not so much an object as a vastly superior force moving you towards them. In other words, it illustrates the shift from an "it starts with me" perspective to a glimpse of that "secondariness" that I've been trying to bring out.

But more specifically: in the illustration that I've just given you, there is a particular moment of awareness which I've referred to as the tipping of the axis. This is the moment when, as you are being shifted into the new perspective, you are able to look back at where you were coming from, and see it in an entirely new light. "Oh my God, to think that I used to think that that was normal and stable! As I move out of that space, I can see what it was really like, something that was really grinding down, sucking me out of being. And what enables me to glimpse this is the hugely more powerful draw, which is pulling me into a much richer and more enlivened space." Simultaneously, there is coming upon you both a sense of delight at what you are becoming, and a sense of shock at how wrong you were about what you now find yourself leaving behind. You are on the dynamic cusp of something where two different realities are peeling away from each other: one is spinning round on itself, turning down into futility and nothingness; while the other, inside which you are beginning to discover yourself, is being spun open into a richer and more demanding participation in the life of something beyond itself.

3. A non-moralistic account of sin and original sin

Well, one of my reasons for giving you this planetary image, which, like all such images, is severely inadequate, is because it brings out something which can very easily get lost in presentations of Christianity. When we talk about what Jesus came to do, did and is doing in our midst, *we are talking about what comes upon us as an alteration of the axis of Creation rather than as a resolution of a moral problem.* Our being brought close into the life of God by Jesus living out being a forgiving victim in our midst has this as its effect: that we perceive simultaneously where we used to be heading, into an ever-shrinking world run by revenge, envy and death; and where we are instead finding ourselves drawn: into being forgiven, forgiving, and thus being opened up into true, insider knowledge of creation as it unfolds dynamically.

In the order of apparent logic, an "it" God created an "it" world in which we then find ourselves, do something wrong, and need forgiving, by an "it" intervention which puts things right. In the order of discovery we only discover the beginning through our experience in the middle: "I AM" is determined to make alive in us the wonder of being God, and so decides to involve us on the inside of creation. Our access to being drawn into this insider status is as we discover ourselves "being forgiven", having our basic paradigm for being human together undone from within by our forgiving victim hoicking us into a richer draw, or pattern of desire, than that which used to run us. From within this richer draw we can see the futility of what we were holding onto before. We were in fact resisting being created, while holding on instead to our futile security; we were locked into a way of being less than human, one that depends on making victims.

So, in fact, in our case, *being forgiven is prior to being created*. This is really what the very ancient Christian doctrine of "Original Sin" teaches. Far from it being a moralistic doctrine, based on dodgy palaeontology and insufficient knowledge of genetics, it is the insistence on that very delicate "backward glance from the cusp of the new creation" as vital to any understanding of who we are finding ourselves to be and how we should behave. To bring out what I mean by how non-moralistic this is, let's go back to our complacent ruler on the planet.

In that image which I gave you, there are two quite different understandings of sin at work, and they are both operative simultaneously. There is the sense of sin as worked out and held onto by the complacent ruler, the one by which the people on the planet were controlled. This sense of sin, naturally enough, depends on the ruler starting from a stable sense of how things are, how they must be, and therefore what is right and what is wrong. If you like, its starting point is obvious. Provided you're the ruler.

The second sense of sin comes from a very odd place. It comes from the sense of shock which all those on the planet undergo as they find themselves summoned up into the new draw. They are enabled, from their new and entirely unexpected vantage point, to glance back at what they had thought of as stable and normal, and see that far from being stable and normal, it had gradually been tilting over backwards into the maw of the black hole. So part of the sense of shock, which is also one of delight, is the realization that they had in fact been completely self-deceived about what was really going on, what was really running them, what was right and what was wrong.

Their reaction is something like this: "Wow! To think that we used to think that living like *that* was normal! Only now are we beginning to get a sense of how small and narrow were the confines of what we thought of as goodness, badness, righteousness, sin and who got to judge us, to give us our criteria. How impotent we were within that framework! It's only now, from the seriously *unstable* seeming, but in fact massively *safe* place of finding ourselves hoicked into a completely new orbit that we begin to get a sense of what's really going on, who we really are, what we are really becoming. Even our quite accurate sense that we often fall short of what we are really becoming looks quite unlike whatever it was that we thought of as sin in our previous orbit."

I hope it is apparent to you that of these two senses of sin, it is only the latter which has a real claim to being part of the Christian faith. And in case you think I'm making this up, rather than being the boringly predictable Catholic theologian that I think I am, then here is the huge star describing the effect of the draw which will start to affect those on the planet as its axis tilts:

> "It is to your advantage that I go away, for if I do not go away, the Defence Counsellor will not come to you. But if I go, I will send him to you. And when he comes he will prove the world wrong about sin and righteousness and judgment; about sin, because they do not believe in me, about righteousness because I'm going to the Father and you will see me no longer; about judgment because the ruler of this world has been judged."[23]

It could scarcely be clearer: there was a notion of sin, and righteousness and judgement that was proper to our world. And it was a notion in which the prosecuting counsel, the accuser, always tended to win. However, in the

---

[23] John 16.7–11.

light of the draw from the huge star, a draw which goes as far as to call itself the Counsel for the Defence, our whole understanding of what sin is, what righteousness looks like and what judgement consists in will be completely reshaped.

And the reason for this change around is not arbitrary: it turns out that the victim of this world's judgement, sense of righteousness, and definition of sin was God himself. Those who perceive this, those who find themselves able to recognize what was going on in the putting to death of Jesus – which means those who find themselves starting to look at themselves from the perspective of their own victim who is in fact forgiving them – those people are receiving a totally new perspective on what sin, righteousness and judgement look like, a perspective which flows towards them from the regard of the forgiving victim. In this perspective, *sin is known in its being forgiven.*

4. The beginning in the middle – Luke

Now that we have explored some of the dimensions of that sense of "secondariness" which I mentioned, I think we are in a good position to look at some of the narrative ways in which the New Testament brings out how it was that a particular human intervention in history was in fact the fulcrum which tips the axis. The fulcrum by which the Creator involves us as active participants in creation. We'll look at Luke first, and then John.

You may remember that in the Book of Genesis, when creation is still formless, and before there is any light, the Spirit moves over the face of the waters.[24] Later God creates Adam, but after a short time Adam and Eve succumb to receiving their sense of "secondariness" through the eyes of the serpent, rather than through the eyes of God, and so start to imagine God as having been in rivalry with them. This leads to the act of disobedience in which they try to become what they were always meant to be, gods, but do so in rivalry with God rather than allowing themselves to become gods held in gracious secondariness by God. They need to grasp what is good and evil for themselves. And then to protect and hide themselves rather than trust the goodness of what they have been given and are. From this, everything starts to wind down. Shortly before they are driven out from Eden, this prophecy is made:

> *"In the sweat of your face you shall eat bread till you return to the ground, for out of it you were taken; you are dust and to dust you shall return."*[25]

What we see in St Luke's Passion narrative, in the route to Jesus' Crucifixion, is Genesis run backwards. After Jesus' last eating of bread, he moves to the place by the Mount of Olives which other Evangelists call Gethsemani (though Luke doesn't). There he prays:

> *"Father, if you wish, take away this cup from me, nevertheless, not my will, but yours be done."* [26]

---

[24] Genesis 1.1–2.
[25] Genesis 3.19.
[26] Luke 22.42.

Rather than this being an insight into the psychology of the one praying, which is how modern readers are inclined to see it, I suggest that what is going on here is Jesus standing in for Adam. He is putting right what Adam got wrong: the human pattern of desire, or will, is being drawn in once more to the Father's pattern of desire. Shortly thereafter we get this:

> And being in agony he prayed more earnestly, and his sweat became like clots of blood falling down upon the ground. [27]

Hidden from us by our translations are a series of Hebrew puns, concerning blood, earth and Adam, all of which are associated with the word *dam*. It is not that Jesus was sweating blood, but that the definitive Adam's sweat, combined with reddish dust, that of the earth, *looked* like clots of blood, returning to the earth whence it had come. In other words, Luke is indicating that here, the prophecy of Genesis 3 which we saw above, is being fulfilled. Adam's being bound down into futility is being undone by the definitive Adam getting right what the first Adam got wrong. Jesus then moves towards his Crucifixion. On the cross he indicates to the criminal who was being executed alongside him, and whom we call the "good thief":

> "Truly, I say to you, today you will be with me in Paradise." [28]

---

[27] Luke 22.44.
[28] Luke 23.43.

This should be taken rather literally, as referring to the Garden before the Fall. The sense that the Book of Genesis is running backwards is brought out even more clearly in the next verses:

> It was now about the sixth hour, and there was darkness over the whole land until the ninth hour, while the sun's light failed;[29]

In other words, the order of creation is running backwards, until we are prior to the moment when God made light. At that moment, and it could not be more appropriate, the symbol of the distinction between God creating everything out of nothing, and the beginning of materiality, of everything that is, is torn:

> And the curtain of the temple was torn in two.[30]

Now we are back at Genesis 1, before anything was created, and at this point:

> Then Jesus, crying with a loud voice, said "Father into thy hands I commit my Spirit!" And having said this he breathed his last.[31]

So finally, we are back to the Spirit hovering over the formless void of Genesis 1. But please notice what has happened. In the Genesis story, the Spirit is impersonal. By the time that Jesus breathes out his Spirit, the Spirit has a fully anthropological content. The Spirit of the Creator actually has shape: what the Creator looks like while creating is not what it appears to be from Genesis – an outside force

---

[29] Luke 23.44.
[30] Luke 23.45.
[31] Luke 23.46.

arranging and ordering things out of some sort of formless-
ness. What the Creator Spirit looks like, and is, is the pattern of desire of one who, in order to make it possible for us
to live, occupies the space of being a dead person for us;
one who has given themselves into the space of being a
dead person before us out of love. This is not a space of
"control" or "ordering" in any obvious sense for any of us.
On the contrary, the power of the Creator has shown itself
as personal in offering us the possibility of becoming persons from a position of complete powerlessness.

When Pentecost comes, a few weeks later, it comes as
the full panoply of the New Creation, starting from a new,
veil-less temple, which is now going to be made up of all
humanity from every language, tribe and nation who are
being empowered to become humans through the presence in their midst of the open heavens, in whose midst,
and constantly available to them, is the utterly alive
Forgiving Victim.

Please notice what has happened: the real beginning
has made itself present in what for us is the middle. This
appearance of the real beginning in the middle looks like,
and is, a painful upheaval. Especially since it is the ability
to occupy the space of shame and death which is what has
tipped the axis of creation. But those who are able to occupy that space are in fact undergoing the shift of planetary
axis such that the real beginning, which is also the real
purpose or end of everything, is being made real in them

now. Here is St Paul making the same point in his own language:[32]

> *I consider that the sufferings of this present time are not worth comparing with the glory that is to be revealed to us. For the creation waits with eager longing for the revealing of the sons of God; for the creation was subjected to futility, not of its own will but by the will of him who subjected it in hope; because the creation itself will be set free from its bondage to decay and obtain the glorious liberty of the children of God. We know that the whole creation has been groaning in travail together until now; and not only the creation, but we ourselves, who have the first fruits of the Spirit, groan inwardly as we wait for adoption as sons, the redemption of our bodies.*

I hope you can see the sense of living on the cusp of two realities: creation is referred to as something which has been opened up and which is drawing us in to it with great zest. And at the same time as something which turns out to have been spinning round and turning in on itself in futility, unaware of what it was destined to become. The axis-turning moment, which is the present moment, in which we are living, feels like an upheaval full of suffering, which is in fact an act of childbirth. Through it, the Creator, "I AM" is bringing into being secondary I AMs, sons and daughters, the "gods" we were promised we would be, as our very bodies are drawn into being insider sharers of the life of God.

---

[32] Romans 8.18–23.

5. The beginning in the middle – John

Now let us look at how St John narrates this same sense
of a futile creation winding down, and the real creation
happening now. In chapter 20, after the crucifixion and
burial of Jesus, it is now the first day of the week. So here
too we are being tipped off that what is about to be
described is somehow linked to the early verses of Genesis.
And this impression is deepened by the fact that there is,
as yet, no light: "it was still dark." After Peter and the
beloved disciple have visited the tomb, and seen that it is
empty, they go home. Mary, however, stands weeping outside the tomb, and then stoops to look inside. What she
sees there are two angels in white, sitting where the body
of Jesus had lain, one at the head and one at the feet. So,
in John, it is not the veil of the temple that is torn, thus
transporting us outside the realm of creation. Rather, the
open tomb turns out to be the now vacated Holy of Holies.
In the Holy of Holies, the seraphim were on either side of
the Mercy Seat, which was where the Presence of God
rested. This is exactly where the angels are in John, except
that they are now resting beside a vacated Mercy Seat. The
Presence is elsewhere. The angels, reasonably enough,
wonder why Mary is weeping. After all, from their point of
view, Eve is now inside the garden again, for the Holy of
Holies and the garden are the same thing. Eve had been
excluded from the garden, and cherubim armed with
swords which turned this way and that had been posted

over the entrance. That would be motive for weeping. But that exclusion from the Garden has now been undone.

Nevertheless, here in this scene of staggered vision, where nothing is quite as it seems, Mary Magdalene doesn't exactly know where she is, confusing this place with a place in which there might actually be a dead person to find. She turns, and sees an unrecognizable Jesus, who addresses her as "Woman" – or Eve. She wonders whether it is the gardener, or Adam. It might also be YHWH wandering in the garden in the cool of the day. And it is indeed both of these, but not as she could imagine them. But then Jesus addresses her by her name, Mary, and she recognizes who he is by what she hears. She turns again. In fact, in this narrative, she is like the sword of the cherubim from Genesis, turning every which way. Nevertheless, what she hears is still part of what was before his death – she hears, and responds to "My teacher". So we are still not quite yet in the New Creation.

This is brought out when Jesus tells her "Do not touch me." You may remember that in Genesis, God told the earthling, before he was divided into Adam and Eve, that he could eat of every tree except the tree of the knowledge of good and evil. God didn't mention anything at all about not touching it. However, when the serpent enquires of Eve about what God had said, Eve has managed to embellish the instruction somewhat:[33]

---

[33] Genesis 3.2–3.

"We may eat of the fruit of the trees of the garden; but God said, 'You shall not eat of the fruit of the tree which is in the midst of the garden, neither shall you touch it, lest you die.'"

In her enthusiasm, she has added the bit about not touching the tree. So in John's Garden, Jesus is taking her back to before that time, undoing Eve's confused excitement. In this staggered vision of Genesis running down, he is still something of a corpse which, according to Numbers 19, should not be touched. Still something of an object rather than pure protagonism. He is not yet the Forgiving Victim who can show his hands and side. It is only when he has gone to his Father that he will open up the space of the New Creation completely, Genesis will cease to run backwards, and everything can move forward.

And so it is, towards the end of the first day, that we come to the room behind closed doors where the disciples are meeting. This first day now stretches backwards from an evening in Jerusalem until the beginning of the second chapter of Genesis, for that is the day that is at last being brought to fruition. And in the midst of the room, in the midst not of myth or of narratives from the past, but of history and fear and tension, the Lord God appears. First he announces peace, then he reveals his hands and his side – this is the Forgiving Victim, the Lamb slaughtered before the foundation of the world. Then he announces peace again. Then he says "As the Father has sent me, so I send you." The beginning has become contemporary, creation is now. And to prove this, Jesus then breathes into the disciples. The word is exactly the same word by which, in Genesis 2.7,[34] the Lord God breathes into the nostrils of earthling, who thus becomes a living being. Here, however, the breath which is breathed into them is described not as "breath of life" but as "Holy Spirit" and with it the ability to forgive or to hold. In other words, exactly as with Luke, it turns out that the Spirit from creation is in fact the Spirit of the Forgiving Victim, and that it is in the degree to which we allow ourselves to be enlivened by the Spirit of the Forgiving Victim that we participate as insiders in the opening out of creation.

This sense of the cusp between the old way of being, fading away, and the new is shown by the parallelism between Mary Magdalene, who can't recognize Jesus clearly, who hears his voice, calls him "My Master" and is urged not to touch him yet, and Thomas who, a full week into the New Creation, sees him, recognizes him clearly thanks to the wounds of the Forgiving Victim, is then invited to touch him, and calls him "My Lord and my God". Furthermore, the touching takes the form of Thomas placing his hand in the side. And in Genesis, just in case we had forgotten, it is from Adam's side that a portion is taken and filled out with flesh. Those who receive the breath, and live according to the Spirit of the Forgiving Victim, are

---

[34] Gen 2.7 and John 20.22: ἐνεφύσησεν

in fact becoming the flesh of the New Adam – Creation is strictly contemporary.

Well, what I've wanted to bring out from these central Christian texts is how removed they are from seeing "Creation" as having been "a long time ago" and God as only intervening moralistically among us by Jesus' death, some time later, to sort out the problem of sin. The early Christian texts show something much richer than that: the true narrative of creation is to be found in the account of Jesus death and resurrection, where the definitive Adam emerges as forgiving victim, thus opening up the possibility of our sharing in something utterly non-futile – creation. At the same time we can see everything which came before as folding back on itself in futility, the off-kilter planet being sucked into the maw of a black hole while all along it was being reached towards in hope by a future of which it had no idea. The forgiveness of our sins, rather than being in the first instance a moralistic matter, is what it looks like for us that the Deathless One has opened up the battened-down culture which eventually makes outsiders of us all; the Forgiving Victim dares us to aspire to be valued insiders in the adventure of creation, starting from our place on the cusp of the shifting axis. From Mrs O'Reilly's perspective, forgiving Johnny was scarcely on her mind at all in the depth of her concern for him, her longing that he be able to share something much bigger with her. For little Johnny, locked in fear and resentment at what he'd done, allowing himself to be forgiven was the *sine qua non* of his being on the inside of the new "we" at all.

6. The gentleness of vision: the grandeur in the everyday

There is something peace-inspiring about images of the sheer hugeness of something coming into our ken. Like the sense of peace and majesty which comes upon those wrestling with the rigging of a small sailing vessel as a huge ocean liner comes alongside. However where my planetary image is weak is that the peace is given off by the imperturbable hugeness of an impersonal "it" rather than being part of what we receive from the imperturbable hugeness of "I AM" coming toward us.

Cast your mind back to the defining moment of creation in St John's Gospel: it comes when the Presence appears in, irrupts into, the locked room where the frightened disciples had gathered. The Presence announces "Peace" before, and after, showing himself. Completely swathed in the peace, out of which he has emerged, he shows his hands and side. By showing himself, non-verbally, in this way "I AM" identifies himself as the Risen Victim, dwelling in the midst of, coming from, and giving off, all the peace that comes from before the foundation of the world. I AM then breathes life into the disciples: the Holy Spirit, which turns out to be the contagion of forgiveness flowing from the Risen Victim who is forgiveness.

What I would like to bring out here is the strange confluence of hugeness and banality in what is going on. The
culminating theophany, in which the very Presence of
YHWH, the Creator, allows itself to be glimpsed in most
finely tuned form as "I AM the Forgiving Victim from
before the foundation of the world"; the fullest vision of all
the power, splendour, weight, gravity, hugeness and
majesty of the heavenly Presence creating humans; this
takes place not on some suitably majestic mountain, nor
even in a gloriously arrayed Temple Sanctuary but instead
in a hideaway, whose locked status "for fear of the Jews" is
almost a parody of the veiled Holy Place of the Temple.

This strange confluence of hugeness and the apparent
banality of the everyday seems to me to be central to our
understanding of what is meant by Incarnation. You may
remember that in Essay 6 I pointed out to you some of
the ways in which Luke depicts Mary, Jesus' mother. This
ordinary girl with marriage plans finds herself invited to
be the portal through which creation out of nothing takes
place, to be in historical fact what had been symbolized
by the Tabernacle overshadowed by the Presence of the
Most High.[35] When pregnant Mary goes to visit her more
heavily pregnant cousin Elizabeth – and what could be
more domestic? – the unborn John the Baptist dances in
her womb, as David danced before the Ark of the

---

[35] The verb here translated as "overshadowed" is the same in Luke
1.35 and in Exodus 40.35, the description of the Tabernacle.

Covenant, and Elizabeth cries out in the voice of the Levites recognizing the Ark. Soon, the family goes to the Temple in Jerusalem for the most simple of rites, and only two aged weirdos, Anna and Simeon, see what has really happened: God has come suddenly to his Temple, fulfilling what the prophet Malachi had foretold, while of course the priests and temple authorities are far too busy keeping the show on the road to perceive the de-centred theophany.

The fascinating thing about the New Testament account is that it does not puff up the Virgin Mary by projecting her backwards, making her as glorious as the Temple artefacts of yesteryear, using her to reinstate them, as it were. On the contrary, it is as though we need to be led out of our fascination with the sacred kitsch of yesteryear if we are to be able to perceive irrupting in our midst, in and as history, all the real weight and glory to which, as we suppose, those artefacts once pointed. In an ordinary theatre production, the initial rehearsals are done in street clothes, with more and more costumes and props being prepared as the rehearsals develop, leading up to all being made ready for the dress rehearsal, where full make-up is worn, and then finally, the first and subsequent performances are enacted with the full panoply of kitsch passing as what is real. The incarnation of YHWH into history follows the exact reverse route: the kitsch and the make-up was all in the rehearsals, and is more and more stripped down the closer we get to the real enactment. The real thing happens in street clothes, and in a way that the set-designers and prop-managers could scarcely recognize. The true grandeur is more visible in the apparent banality of this off-centre acting out than ever it was among the theatre props of old.

And here it really is worth our while to spend a little time with Mary, for if there is any way at all that we can understand the things I've been trying to point towards here, it is in her company. Her personal history is one of being stretched out of myth and into history. There is a continuity between the old creation and the new, between the Old Israel, and its institutions, and the new, and it is lived out by Mary being stretched by what is done in her as she provides the flesh for the Lord God to come among his people; and then in what is done *to* her as the Lord God works among his people. She is the first, and most complete, example of that "secondariness" that I've been trying to bring out in this essay, receiving who she is through the regard of the Presence which has come into history through her.

In Luke's Gospel, where she enters the story as the moment when all the artefacts and prophecies become history, she very quickly moves to being the one who is told that a sword will pierce her heart, and as things develop "she stores all these things in her heart." Later she undergoes a further being stretched: her own apparent relativization at the hands of her son:

> *Then his mother and his brothers came to him, but*
> *they could not reach him because of the crowd.*
> *And he was told, "Your mother and your brothers*
> *are standing outside, wanting to see you." But he*
> *said to them, "My mother and my brothers are*
> *those who hear the word of God and do it."* [36]

Only someone who was very secure in being held in their secondariness could undergo such an experience without wanting to grasp onto being special. But she is not in rivalry with the huge elective family that her son is bringing into being, not humiliated by the evident collapse of generations into one single contemporary generation which Jesus is producing.

At the beginning of Acts we glimpse her again. At first she is named as one of the group who gather for prayer after Jesus' Ascension, but before Pentecost. But by the day of Pentecost, she, like all the others, is included but no longer named: "they were all together in one place." For those who are born again on Pentecost are all of the same generation. Her motherhood of Jesus has been stretched into her being sister of her son's new sisters and brothers. The one who provided the raw material for the New Creation has become an insider within that new creation.

Or, as Dante says it: [37]

---

[36] Luke 8.19–21.
[37] The first lines of Canto XXXIII of Dante's *Paradiso*.

Vergine Madre, figlia del tuo figlio,
umile e alta più che creatura,
termine fisso d'etterno consiglio,
tu se' colei che l'umana natura
nobilitasti sì, che 'l suo fattore
non disdegnò di farsi sua fattura.

Maiden yet a Mother, daughter of your son; at once the most humble of creatures yet higher than them all; for in you the plan from before all time rests as in its final end; So much did you ennoble human nature, that its creator had no second thoughts about becoming its creature.

John tells us the same thing in a slightly different way. In the immediate run-up to Jesus' death several things happen as the ancient Atonement rite is fulfilled by being stretched out of theatre and into history. Jesus' garments are divided among the soldiers, except for his tunic, which is explicitly described as without seam, and woven from top to bottom. This is a description of the High Priestly garment woven in the same way as the Temple Veil. Over this garment, the soldiers cast lots, reminding us that the High Priest would have cast lots to decide which of the unblemished lambs would get to stand in for YHWH and which for Azazel.

Shortly after this moment, Jesus is going to announce that he thirsts, and will be given vinegar to drink, thus bringing together the way in which the priests consumed the "portion of the Lord" – the entrails of the lamb they had slaughtered – with the help of vinegar. And he will then announce "it is completed" or "finished" or "consummated" or "settled by sacrifice" – all of these translations bring out elements which underlie Jesus' last word in John's Gospel.

In between these two moments in which Jesus fulfilled elements of the rite, there is an apparent interlude, in which Jesus' mother, his mother's sister, Mary the wife of Clopas, Mary Magdalene and the beloved disciple are found standing close to the cross. A mixture of people from both Jesus' family of birth and his elective family.

> *When Jesus saw his mother, and the disciple whom he loved standing near, he said to his mother, "Woman, behold, your son!" Then he said to the disciple, "Behold, your mother!" And from that hour the disciple took her to his own home.* [38]

This exchange is often read as though Jesus were addressing his mother, pointing her, perhaps with a slight nod of the head, towards the beloved disciple, who, he thus indicates, should now be treated by her as her son. He then addresses the beloved disciple, and, again, with a nod of his head, indicates to the disciple that Mary should now be treated as his mother. I wonder, however, whether that is really what is going on here. It would be very much part of John's style to be indicating something rather richer than a little last moment "family arrangements for when I'm gone" scene.

It would make much more sense to me if, within this scene by the cross, John is exploring the image of "travail", or birth-giving, which he used before when Jesus was preparing his disciples for his forthcoming execution:

---

[38] John 19.26–27.

"Truly, truly, I say to you, you will weep and lament, but the world will rejoice; you will be sorrowful, but your sorrow will turn into joy. When a woman is in travail she has sorrow, because her hour has come; but when she is delivered of the child, she no longer remembers the anguish, for joy that a child is born into the world. So you have sorrow now, but I will see you again and your hearts will rejoice, and no one will take your joy from you." [39]

If that is the case, then I wonder whether it isn't better to read both the uses of "behold" in the scene by the cross as drawing the eyes of the person being addressed *to Jesus*. He is urging his mother whom he here greets as "Woman" as though she were Eve, to behold him, her son. In doing so he is both indicating the old creation going out of being which is killing her son, and indicating to her that she is in travail with him for a birthing that is taking place now. Then he draws the eyes of the beloved disciple towards himself *as mother* indicating that in his going to death he is bringing to birth a new family. From that hour a new family is being born, and it makes perfect sense for the relationship of Mary and the beloved disciple to be recast as one in which they are of the same generation. The elective family which has been brought into being by Jesus' birthing stretches towards and welcomes into it the woman whose motherhood was both honoured and yet had its cultural meaning transformed as it was stretched into a sisterhood in the new creation.

[39] John 16.20–22.

Isaiah had already foreseen something along these lines in a passage to which the image of "travail" seems to refer:

> *"Before she was in labour she gave birth; before her pain came upon her she was delivered of a son. Who has heard such a thing? Who has seen such things? Shall a land be born in one day? Shall a nation be brought forth in one moment? For as soon as Zion was in labour she brought forth her sons."*[40]

This sense of Jesus himself being involved in giving birth, producing the new generation of those who are on a complete level of equality with himself, is further brought out when, after his death, a soldier pierces his side with a spear:

> *And at once there came out blood and water.*[41]

This is remarkably like the appearance of afterbirth. If this were not enough, then we can be sure that John is trying to show us that a new kind of family has been brought into existence by these events, since when Jesus speaks to Mary Magdalene in the garden, he tells her:

> *"Do not hold me, for I have not yet ascended to the Father; but go to my brethren and say to them, I am ascending to my Father and your Father, to my God and your God."*[42]

This is the first time in the Gospel that Jesus refers to his brethren as "my brethren". More significantly, while he has frequently referred to God as his Father, never before in John's Gospel was there any indication that God was

---

[40] Isaiah 66.7–8.
[41] John 19.34b.
[42] John 20.17.

properly speaking the father of anyone else. In going to his death, having become the mother of the new generation of brethren, he has opened out the possibility for them to be sons and daughters of God, for God to be their Father in exactly the same way that he was Jesus' Father.

However, please notice, once again, that what has happened is that all the grandeur of creation has erupted quietly into some very subtle changes of relationship among very ordinary people. And this is a constant throughout the Gospels. What is being birthed is a new family, one in which the elective has a huge priority over the biological. In this new family, there are no fathers, and no one is to be called father. Biological progenitors are inter-generational brothers. Cultural paternity is very much part of the planet that was winding down into futility, part of the reach into our lives of the maw of the black hole that was sucking us out of being.

Instead we find ourselves being brought into a new family, all of the same generation. All of us sisters and brothers who are becoming secondary beacons of I AM, which means to say, all of us finding ourselves living out being sons and daughters of the Father as we learn to live out being sisters and brothers to each other. And we find that Jesus is both in the midst of us as Presence, in whose regard we are beginning to glow; and we are in the midst of him, becoming him, without thereby being displaced, or becoming any less ourselves.

Furthermore this creation of a new family doesn't happen by decree, anonymously. It happens by ordinary, named individuals finding themselves drawn out, thanks to the words and examples of other named individuals, from being tied down into the various forms of cultural togetherness going nowhere to which we so often attribute such a sacred worth. Instead, they find themselves, over time, undergoing the process of being adopted into a new, elective family, which may even include some of their family of birth, but with the relationships quite transformed.

This happens slowly, gently, and with enormous patience and affection, since what looks like an enormous upheaval for us, is only the space needed for God's smile to break through the sadness of our angry futility. This, for me, is one of the reasons why it is so good to remember the slowness, the gentleness, the stretchedness of the regard of God who brings into being with joy. This regard is most memorably reflected back on us by the presence within the new family, sometimes called the communion of saints, of our living sister, the Mother of God – she who birthed the One who birthed her. A gentleness and a patience undergirded with joy by which, even in the midst of violence, murder and mayhem, she patiently helps us undo the knots that tie us into the old creation, so as to help us come to reflect the new.

But please don't be put off by the pious-sounding language of the "communion of saints". This is simply a way of referring to the elective family of named persons within history who know and like each other, starting within very ordinary sets of relationships. These people have found that all the joy of the new creation has been birthed in them as they have undergone a shift in their relationships with each other, empowered by the forgiving victim to step out of rivalry, revenge and resentment in all its glorious-seeming cultural masks, and instead to run the risk of being held together only by the light that flows from the Lamb.

> *"Truly I tell you, there is no one who has left house or brothers or sisters or mother or father or children or fields, for my sake and for the sake of the good news, who will not receive a hundredfold now in this age – houses, brothers and sisters, mothers and children, and fields, with persecutions – and in the age to come eternal life. But many who are first will be last, and the last will be first."*[43]

I hope it is clear how all that we have been looking at here is of a piece with something we glimpsed in Essay 2. We saw two disciples, one named, Cleophas, and one unnamed, walking on the road to Emmaus. I wanted to call the unnamed disciple "N", or "Name to be supplied" so that any one of us can inscribe our name into the story alongside Cleophas.

I hope that you can now see that "N" matters more than may have seemed to be the case. Luke was not setting out

---

[43] Mark 10.29–31.

a formal recipe for the involvement of yet-to-be-named individuals in an automatic mechanism. He was setting out an invitation by which we may find ourselves as named members of a real family, creating real and lasting ties, discovering who we really are around the presence of the Forgiving Victim. The One who, in revealing himself to us, not only enlightens us, but lightens us up into being transmitters both of lightness and of light.

ESSAY TWELVE

Neighbours and insiders:

What's it like to dwell in a non-moralistic commandment?

Introduction

We have at least reached the final stretch of our course, the one where I told you that I would trespass onto the terrain of morality. You will agree, I hope, that up until now I have avoided not only morality, but even the appearance of morality. From the beginning I have been trying to insist on something which every presenter of the Christian faith knows in principle, which is that Christianity is a religion of grace, not of laws or morals.

Often enough, and unfortunately, however, presentations of the Christian faith collapse back fairly quickly into pointing people towards a religion of laws, or morals. One in whose basic storyline God created everything good, humans fell, and then Jesus came to put that right. That's usually the moment when grace appears in the story. However, in some presentations, after Jesus has put everything right, then really all that is left for us to do is to behave well according to a pre-existing code which we must just accept. After an initial conversion experience, such "grace" as we might encounter about the place is in fact a supposed power enabling weak-willed individuals to stick to pre-established rules.

I hope that it is by now obvious to you that a presentation of this sort is not helpful. An account of faith which postulates a mysterious event in the past leading to painful morals in the present reveals its distance from the original by making Christianity boring. And that, above all, is the trap that I've been trying to avoid. Instead of this, I have been attempting to set before you a rather different take on the same events. One in which a rambunctiously Alive One – the one I have described as "the Other other", effervescent beyond words – comes rushing towards us, taking us by surprise, undoing us from bonds we scarcely knew were there, and bringing us to life.

In this picture, it's the Alive One, who turns out to be drawing us in to himself, who opens us up to the realization that where we were before was dangerously out of kilter. In this picture creation, rather than being a boring "given" somewhere in the background, is something towards which we find ourselves being fascinatingly drawn. Drawn from a "not yet" that is both given and beyond us, rather than an "already fixed" that is behind us. And our route from the "dangerously out of kilter" place of something constantly tending to futility, towards the rich, fascinating, solid "not yet" that is opening up for us, passes through the breaking open of our hearts. For that breaking open of our heart so as to make room for a larger heart is the effect in our lives of the forgiveness of sins.

In this picture, it's the new way of being which is coming upon us which leads to a new way of behaving. And that is very much the approach to be found in the New Testament. In Paul's letters, the approach is not "do X, and then you will become Y", it is rather, "Because you are finding yourselves X, so do Y." So for instance:

> If then you have been raised with Christ, seek the things that are above, where Christ is, seated at the right hand of God. Set your minds on the things that are above, not on the things that are on earth. For you have died, and your life is hid with Christ in God. When Christ who is our life appears, then you will also appear with him in glory. Put to death therefore what is earthly in you. [44]

The understanding is pretty clear: something happens that takes us somewhere quite new. As we find ourselves on the inside of the new life, allowing our imaginations to be rejigged, so the ways of behaving which flow from that

---

[44] Colossians 3.1–5. Paul argues similarly in Romans 6.3–14.

new life become second nature to us, and we are able to ditch those which don't flow from that new life. It is what we are becoming that is first, and the transformation of our behaviour which flows from that.

This makes sense to me: it is as I discover myself on the inside of a new way of being that I discover the sense, and the richness, of different ways of behaving. And indeed, we find ourselves on the inside of discovering for ourselves quite why these new ways of behaving correspond to the richest and deepest loving intention for us of our Creator. In other words, there is something genuinely exciting about learning to be fascinated by a goodness we didn't know.

And this of course has been the whole burden of this course: how it is that someone coming towards us, and into our midst, catches us by surprise and enables us to be turned into *ourselves-for-each-other*, something much richer and more zest-inspiring than we could guess while we thought we knew who we were. The very reverse of boring!

1. WWJD

So in order to kick-start our look at the shape of good living which flows from the Christian faith, I'm going to be polemical with a little tag, which is often used as a sort of a quick guide to Christian morality. The tag is "What Would Jesus Do?" Many of you will have heard this before. In fact, there was a period when many people wore bangles or wristbands with "WWJD" inscribed on them, as a reminder of their moral compass. I've been told that though these wristbands were very popular in the United States before the events of September 11th 2001, their sales declined precipitously thereafter. Presumably because it was pretty clear that blind revenge, pre-emptive warfare, legitimating torture, and lying about weapons of mass destruction were not What Jesus Would Do.

But, to the phrase itself: "What Would Jesus Do?" I think it has a certain positive value, since, as a moral guide, its first demand is that you should remember stories. Any answer to "What would Jesus do?" is always going to take the questioner back to stories in which Jesus interacts with people. "Jesus would do what he did with the woman taken in adultery, or with the money changers in the Temple, or with his executioners, or he would act according to the stories he told about the two people praying in the Temple, or the Good Samaritan, or the Prodigal Son." This, as I understand it, is the positive value of asking "What Would Jesus Do?": it pushes us into remembering stories, into thinking our way into situations with the help of the memories of those stories.

However, there is also, I think, a less helpful element to the tag, and that is because of its implicit presupposition. After all, the phrase "What Would Jesus Do?" is really only half a sentence. The unsaid second half is: "if he were here". In other words, the tag presupposes that Jesus isn't here. And this means that the person who is saying "WWJD" is working out of a space something like this: "Look, I'm on my own, I've got to take responsibility for getting something right, and I've somehow got to work out what Jesus would do if he were here, which he isn't, and then push myself into doing it." I hope you can see that this takes us straight back to a world in which working at morals presumes absence and a straining of the will.

What we'll be looking at, however, is what I would call a presumption of *presence* rather than a presumption of absence. From this perspective the question is not "What Would Jesus Do?", but "What is Jesus doing?", which is of course both a much more difficult, and a much more interesting, question to answer. For the answer to this second question, which might also be framed "What is it like to live according to the Spirit which Jesus is breathing into us?", requires us to be alive to all the kinds of things which we've been looking at through the course. Things like being approached by improbable people with foreign accents on strange roads who turn your story upside down; things like being forgiven, totally unexpectedly, by your victim, and therefore being dragged into reimagining your world as you find yourself being given to be someone you never thought you might become. As you can imagine, thinking through this second question, "What is Jesus doing?", takes much more time, and is not so easy to sort out quickly.

So, what is Jesus doing? By beginning with this presumption of presence, I'm going to explore how we learn to sink into, or develop, a habitual sensitivity to a certain form of imitation, and of being challenged, by the mode of Jesus' presence which we saw when we looked at the Road to Emmaus. As I become acclimatized to this habitual sensitivity, I can learn to discern what Jesus is doing under my current circumstances. Just as he continues to give me his body, entrusting me to take it where I will, to make of it what I will, so I can give my body to him, to carry on doing what he is doing. In doing this, I'm being drawn into a flexible imitation of him. I'm not imitating him mechanically. Rather I'm imitating him creatively: "Oh, yes, I can see that this is what he's doing now, and I'm getting to be on the inside of it. It's just like what he was doing in the past, but in very changed circumstances. The past serves as my reference point, as it were, a banister to hold onto, as I check that I am indeed on the inside of what he's doing now, being carried up into his project; that I am indeed, to use Jesus' own language, his friend, rather than his servant."

2. Luke's testimony: the lawyer's question

To give you a clearer sense of what I'm talking about, we're going to look at the parable of the Good Samaritan.[45] The context of the parable gives us a good frame:

> *Just then a lawyer stood up to put Jesus to the test. "Teacher," he said, "what must I do to inherit eternal life?"*

---

[45] Luke 10.25–37.

"Inheriting eternal life" is a more interesting phrase than it might seem to those of us whose first reaction is that it is a simply another way of saying "what must I do to go to heaven?" Inheriting is what the ultimate insiders did (in those days, sons, but not daughters) and "eternal life" was a way of referring to the life of God. So St Luke frames the parable as a discussion of what it looks like to become an insider in the life of God.

First, the lawyer sets out his challenge: what sort of complex answer will Jesus come up with? In fact Jesus remits the lawyer to something entirely non-esoteric, something entirely public and available to any listener:

> He said to him, "What is written in the law? How
> do you read?"

Knowing perfectly well that the texts of the law can be made to say many things, Jesus asks the lawyer not only *what* the text says, but also *how he* interprets the law.[46] And the lawyer answers very properly, not by quoting a single text, but by putting together two texts from two different books of the Torah. The first is from Deuteronomy 6.5 where it says:

> ... you shall love the Lord your God with all your
> heart, and with all your soul, and with all your
> might.

And the second from Leviticus 19.18 where it says:

---

[46] The Greek, followed by the majority of translations, gives "how do you read?" The NRSV, idiosyncratically, gives "What do you read there?"

... you shall love your neighbour as yourself.

So the lawyer makes an act of legal interpretation, bringing together two laws in such a way that they interpret each other. What it looks like to be on the inside of the life of God is to be stretched towards God with every faculty of your being, and the form this takes is being stretched towards your neighbour.

Jesus commends the lawyer. He is not only a good lawyer, he has a good moral sense as well, since he has made an act of interpretation which, while it was probably not innovative, is, in the different variants in which it has reached us, definitive: he has turned two different commandments into one single commandment which will in fact never be abrogated. Henceforth being on the inside of the life of God and being stretched lovingly towards my neighbour can never be separated. This is not merely a moralistic matter, but shows a firm anthropological insight. What I mean is that we are animals whose "selves" are brought into being through our relationships with others: we are reflexive. So how we treat our neighbours and how we treat ourselves are inescapably linked, and no amount of either apparent egoism or of fake altruism can do anything other than disguise this fact from us! Thus, indeed, our only access to finding ourselves loved is through our learning to love someone else.

And Jesus said to him, "You have answered rightly;
do this, and you will live."

The lawyer however wanted to take the matter further:

> *But wanting to justify himself, he asked Jesus,*
> *"And who is my neighbour?"*

I wonder what Luke means when he says that the lawyer wanted to justify himself? It's a curious phrase, and the sentiment occurs several times in this Gospel with the sense of a person who wants to make themselves good in their own eyes. Here it is not clear whether the lawyer thought he was asking a difficult question and was expecting a more complex answer. Perhaps he was rather underwhelmed when Jesus, having drawn from him a fairly succinct answer to his own question, simply commended him. Imagine: you try to challenge someone with a potentially complex technical question and clearly, by your demeanour and style, expect a detailed answer which will flatter you for being intelligent as well as expose possible weak flanks in your interlocutor's approach to things. Your interlocutor hears you out, and then, after a deep-looking pause, simply answers: "Yes, I agree." Well, it takes the wind out of your sails, and your colleagues giggle at you, the class clever-clogs who tried to catch teacher out, but ended up firmly but gently put in their place.

Or maybe the point of the lawyer's original question — literally "doing what will I inherit eternal life?" — was that he wanted an answer that gave him a specific "what's the legal minimum necessary?" In other words, when Luke says that the lawyer wanted to justify himself, maybe what the lawyer wanted was a more immediately applicable answer to his question, the sort of instruction that someone can "get right", fill in the right boxes, thereby becoming one of the good guys. If that's what he wanted, then an answer that sets out the overall framework, but leaves a huge field for the hard work of interpretation and application to life situations, would not meet his need.

In any case, the lawyer has a follow-up question, and it is by no means stupid. He is not merely asking Jesus to be more specific; he is asking a reasonable legal question about the interpretation of Leviticus 19, whence the second part of his own answer had been drawn. For the verse from which the lawyer had culled the phrase "and your neighbour as yourself" contains more than the part he had quoted. In full it reads:

> *"You shall not take vengeance or bear any grudge against the sons of your own people, but you shall love your neighbour as yourself: I am the LORD."*[47]

Here, the word "neighbour" appears to refer to "the sons of your own people" – fellow Hebrews. What makes the lawyer's question legally interesting is not that the bit of Leviticus which he quotes has a circumscribed meaning, but precisely the reverse: it is the fact that a few verses later in the same chapter of Leviticus, following on a number of commandments to do with intermingling of cattle, sex with slaves, hair trimming, witchcraft, and respect for old age, we get the following:

[47] Leviticus 19.18.

"When a stranger sojourns with you in your land, you shall not do him wrong. The stranger who sojourns with you shall be to you as the native among you, and you shall love him as yourself; for you were strangers in the land of Egypt: I am the LORD your God." [48]

So Leviticus appears to interpret itself, for the same phrase, "you shall love him as yourself", which was previously applied to the word "neighbour", here acquires a new density: the stranger who sojourns among you is declared to be the exact legal equivalent of one of the "sons of your own people", and therefore a neighbour in the strict sense of the commandment. In other words, the text of Leviticus seems to be heading in the direction of the term "neighbour" becoming universal, and that is worrying legally, since if everyone is your neighbour, then the term "neighbour" has no longer got any precise legal meaning at all, and how are you to know if you are obeying a commandment when it has no precise meaning?

So it appears that our lawyer is actually asking Jesus to interpret Leviticus, urging him to flesh out the relationship between being on the inside of the life of God and the discussion concerning applicable forms of neighbourliness. And Jesus agrees to take the matter on.

And taking him up, Jesus said ...

The Greek is interesting, in that of the possible words or phrases for "reply", the one used is not the more contes-

---

[48] Leviticus 19.33–34.

tatory, "in your face" sort of reply, but rather the kind that a legal authority would give who had agreed to take on the matter. In other words, Jesus is not here showing the lawyer up. Rather he's saying, "OK, you're on. Let's see where we can take this." The parable that follows is his acceptance of the challenge simultaneously to show what it is like to be on the inside of the life of God and to interpret Leviticus well in the matter of the neighbour. Let us read it:

> *"A man was going down from Jerusalem to Jericho, and fell into the hands of robbers, who stripped him, beat him, and went away, leaving him half dead.*

So, here is the setting. The man is unspecified. It is not evident that he was a Hebrew. Merely that he was a human. Whatever sort of human he was, he fell into the hands of people who did not discriminate between "sons of your people" and "sojourners in your land" – they were disobedient to Leviticus under any of its interpretations. Their proximity to him was of entirely the wrong sort.

> *Now by chance a priest was going down that road; and when he saw him, he passed by on the other side. So likewise a Levite, when he came to the place and saw him, passed by on the other side.*

I particularly like the word "by chance". It too forms part of the answer to the question. Nothing in Jesus' story is stable, or ordered, everything is fluid and contingent.

Whatever the teaching to be derived from this parable, it will be to do with navigating the fluxes not of what should be, but of what just happens. The priest was, as it happens, going down the road. Interestingly, the road from Jerusalem to Jericho is downhill, so the priest was in fact going away from Jerusalem, and towards Jericho. In other words, he wasn't on his way to his Temple duties in Jerusalem. And the text doesn't tell us anything about the psychology of his motivation in passing by on the other side. It doesn't say that he was disgusted, or a coward, or in a hurry. Merely that he was a priest and that, seeing the wounded one, he passed by on the other side.

There were in fact perfectly respectable reasons for a priest to pass by. The man had been left half dead, and that means that it would not be obvious, without going close to him, and perhaps turning him over, whether he were dead or not. In any case, there was certainly shed blood all over the place. And if you were a priest, you had very important professional reasons to avoid being close to a corpse, or to spilled blood. In fact, central to the whole Holiness Code and the life of the Holy of Holies in the Temple was that it was a place utterly removed from death. The priests, whose ordination included the notion of a "resurrection" by which they became sharers in angelic life, must have nothing to do with corpses, blood, other than that of sacrificial beasts, or corruption. Indeed, a priest's ability to serve God in the Holy Place would have been severely impaired, and

he would have to undergo a complicated series of ablu-
tions, if he had touched an unclean thing. All this is set out
in Leviticus 21 and 22, not at all far from our passage.

So the priest and, similarly but to a lesser extent, the
Levite, both had quite solid motives for giving a wide berth
to the potential corpse by the side of the road. The potential
corpse either might, or definitely would, impede their service of God. In fact, it was an obstacle to being on the inside
of the life of God as enacted liturgically in the Holy Place.
You can imagine them, maybe without any personal sense of
disgust, or fear of corpses, or any psychological issues to do
with hygiene and contagion, thinking, entirely in good con-
science: "I do hope someone else comes by soon to attend to
the poor fellow, if it isn't already too late for him. In fact, if
the mobile phone had been invented, I would call a non-
priestly friend for back-up – but it hasn't been yet. However,
my role in life is clear: it is to serve God in his Holy Place,
and share in his life by my anointed service, and I shouldn't
let this accident, this unfortunate happenstance, upset the
true order of the world, the unruffled stability in which the
Almighty rejoices, and which it is my job to help promote,
so, I'd better pass by on the other side."

Then along comes the Samaritan:

> But a Samaritan while traveling came near him;
> and when he saw him, he was moved with pity.

Now the interesting thing about the Samaritan is that he
is not, from the perspective of the Jewish lawyer, the total-

ly outside "other" – a complete foreigner. He occupies the much more infuriating place of being exactly the wrong sort of other: the one who is sufficiently like us to get us all riled up – a classic trigger for the reaction produced by the narcissism of minor differences. The Samaritans after all, worshipped the same God, with a slightly different, but overlapping, set of Scriptures. They didn't acknowledge Jerusalem as a sacred centre, worshipping instead on Mount Gerizim. So Jews and Samaritans were a perpetual reproach to each other, sources of reciprocal moral infuriation.

Please notice what Jesus is doing here. As part of his picture of what it is like to be on the inside of the life of God, he is nudging his listeners into being stretched out of their comfort zone, into traversing their own hostility, by having to look at the situation through suspect eyes. In other words, built into his story is the same perspective that we saw in our reading of the Road to Emmaus: that the one who will turn out to be the bearer of what is true is the one who seems to us like the sort of person who "wouldn't get it" since they're "not one of us".

Moving along then, immediately the Samaritan draws near the half-dead man, we get the parable's bombshell word: ἐσπλαγχνίσθη – which our translation gives as "was moved with pity". In fact the word is much stronger than that. It means "viscerally moved" and so is much more like our English "was gut-wrenched". What is important here is that this is the Greek form of the word by which God was described as viscerally moved, moved in the entrails or the womb. In other words, right there, in the midst of this happenstance, what it looks like to be on the inside of the life of God has burst forth.

And what it looks like is an entirely different relation to a potential or actual corpse than might have been expected. The priest who had kept himself pure for sacrifice might well find himself in the Temple alongside the corpse of an animal that he had just sacrificed. He might even, depending on which feast it was, find himself having to eat the entrails of the animal in question. For it was the entrails that were known as "the portion of the Lord". By eating them, the priest would be taking part in the life of God. Yet here it is the entrails, the life of God, which burst forth towards the utterly vulnerable victim by the side of the road, in the flesh of the Samaritan who is moved towards him.

> He went to him and bandaged his wounds, having poured oil and wine on them. Then he put him on his own animal, brought him to an inn, and took care of him.

So, first of all, he moves close to him, instead of away from him. Then, using oil to soothe the wounded flesh, and wine which was the basic disinfectant of the period, he bandages the half-dead one, and brings him to an inn. Once he gets to the inn, please notice what he doesn't do. Neither he nor the text make any reference to the ethnicity of the wounded one. He doesn't say to the innkeeper: "Look, I found one of yours on the side of the road, and have done far more than my bit by bringing him here, but now he's your responsibility" – something a foreigner might easily say to a co-national of the wounded one. On the contrary, even being with him in the inn, the Samaritan doesn't pass the buck, but continues to take care of him.

> *The next day he took out two denarii, gave them to the innkeeper, and said, 'Take care of him; and when I come back, I will repay you whatever more you spend.'*

Come the next day, and the Samaritan still doesn't distance himself from the wounded one. Even when he is going to be physically distant about his business, he leaves a generous first instalment with the innkeeper – two days' wages – and pledges himself to make good an open-ended debt, for who can foresee the time necessary for healing, and the possible expenses to be incurred as the result of wounds sustained? In fact, the Samaritan becomes an indefinitely extended source of invisible succour for the wounded one, working through the local ministrations of the innkeeper.

Jesus then addresses the lawyer:

> *Which of these three, do you think, was a neighbour to the man who fell into the hands of the robbers?"*

And even here, his phrasing is most suggestive. The lawyer had asked him "Who is my neighbour?" with the implication that the term "neighbour" referred to the passive object of mandated benevolence: "If we can define who my neighbour is, then I will know towards whom I am obligated to behave in a neighbourly way." But Jesus has it the other way round: the word neighbour refers not to the passive object of the benevolence, mandated or not, but to the active creator of neighbourliness. A further hint that he is answering the question "what is it like to be on the inside of the life of God"?

The lawyer answers Jesus very exactly, and without any reference to the ethnic issues involved:

He said, "The one who showed him mercy."

Please notice, however, that in order to be able to give that very exact answer, he, the lawyer has had to be dragged through all the discomfort of learning to discover real goodness through the viewpoint of someone who was in principle highly suspect. He has had to traverse his own hostility and repugnance in order to have clarity.

Jesus said to him, "Go and do likewise."

In other words: if you want to inherit the life of God, there is no safely circumscribed definition of who your neighbour is. Instead you will find yourself swept up into the inside of an infinitely attentive creation of neighbourliness amidst all the victimary contingencies of human life. And that attentiveness will be refined as you learn to avoid being seduced by sacrificial forms of religious goodness and as you overcome your own formation in the resulting culture of hostility.

3. Luke's testimony: The Samaritan's learning curve

Having looked at the parable from the lawyer's point of view, now we are going to explore it from the perspective of the Samaritan. It was, after all, he who was finding himself on the inside of the life of God. What did it look like for him?

One of the things the parable takes for granted in the midst of contingency is the centrality of victims. Victims appear in two valencies in our story: sacred victims, of the sort to be found in temples, and which inspire certain attitudes towards blood and corpses; and contingent victims, who are to be found in the midst of violent human interactions. We might, following the passage from Hosea[49] at which we looked in Essay 8, call the human attitude towards the first sort "sacrifice", and the human attitude towards the second sort "mercy". Concentrating our attention on the first sort of victim leads to a certain habitual blindness towards the second sort. While attention to the second sort leads to a certain sort of insight concerning the first sort. What is in common is that those involved in both valencies, the priest and levite on the one hand, and the Samaritan, on the other, are drawn by a pattern of desire which is intimately involved with a victim.

---

[49] Hosea 6.6.

So here is the first hint of the shape of being on the inside of the life of God, what it's like to become sensitive to where Jesus is and what he's doing now: there is something ineluctable about what is at its centre. The human pattern of desire is such that we either create goodness by displacing victims, or find ourselves being made good by moving towards them. But a form of goodness which is entirely unrelated to dealing with the human reality of victimhood is not something available to our species. So much is this so that René Girard, with whose understanding of desire we have been working throughout this course, wondered what it was that first led proto-humans to discover the distinctions between "good" and "bad", "in" and "out", "us" and "not-us" which are set into the bedrock of distinctively human culture.

Girard postulates that human culture emerges from an (often repeated) act of lynching amongst groups of proto-humans that came before our construction of goodness and badness. "Good" and "bad", "in" and "out", "us" and "not-us", and all their related culture-sustaining binaries would only have emerged fully within our race as a result of the frenzy of a group's all-against-all yielding to the all-against-one in which anthropoids discovered ourselves as humans. The lack of differentiation of the horde starts to yield to the beginning of regular culture as a source of meaning and structure emerges: the one who is "not us", the one who, being "out", enables us to be "in", the one who thus enables us to sense the "goodness" of what we have done, as they come to be detected as "bad". This does indeed illustrate how the emergent difference that it later became possible to call a "victim" is at the root of our hominization. And how victimhood is an ineluctable reality in our species.

Goodness or badness according to "sacrifice", then, is what enables us to be good by contrast with some defiling other. And goodness or badness according to mercy is discovered in our being moved, or not, to show neighbourliness to one considered defiling. Thus we may find ourselves relating to victimhood in a way that dances around it, as it were, being given an apparently strong identity in our going along with the various forms of fascination with, and repulsion from, victimhood. In this way we will merely be continuing the founding gestures of human culture, seduced by our own lie about the one who "is not us". Or, with much greater difficulty, at least in my case, we can allow ourselves to face the centrality of the victim in a way that is not run by a mixture of fascination and fear, and be given to be who we are to be, starting from our recognition of ourselves in the one who is just there. The attitude to victims is the criterion for neighbourliness.

Let's watch the Samaritan a little. As he comes along the road, he undergoes a certain draw. The verb is passive. His entrails did something to him, they moved him. In fact, he saw the wounded one, entrail to entrail, he saw the altogether too visible entrails of the other as his own, which is, as we have seen, what God does in the Temple sacrifice, with the Lord's portion, the entrails, of the victim. So this is what it is like to find yourself on the inside of the life of God! It means being gut-wrenched by your likeness with vulnerable flesh.

Finding himself on the inside of the life of God means that the Samaritan is able to draw near to the place of death, actual or potential, with no fear. He is not moved by death. It doesn't exercise any draw or fascination for him. The possibility that the person to whom he is drawing close might actually be, or shortly become, a corpse, an instrument of defilement, doesn't concern him. Just as it doesn't concern him that his beast of burden would have been rendered unclean by carrying a bloodied person or a cadaver. Being unmoved by death, he is fully able to draw close to a fellow human being without fear.

Let us think through this attitude to death a little more. It does seem to be completely central to how we understand being on the inside of the life of God. For in the parable, we are dealing with two approaches to the same reality: the deathlessness of God. In the one approach, God's deathlessness is somehow thought to need protecting. Protecting in two senses: protecting against, because thought to be a hugely violent and unstable reality that might swamp mere humans with wrath; and protecting from contamination, as though God's deathlessness would somehow be diminished if allowed to be brought close to corruption and mortality.

In the other approach, the deathlessness of God is such that it is not in rivalry in any way at all with the reality of death. It is able to move towards, and around, and with, mortal beings and mortal remains without in any sense being weakened by them. On the contrary. It is the deathlessness of God which gives life to mortal things. So, faced with a half-dead stranger on a road, one understanding of deathlessness interprets the half-dead one as on the way to death, and thus to be shunned, while the other interprets the half-dead one as able to be brought to life, and thus to be nurtured.

In Jesus' resurrection, God demonstrated to us, fully, firmly, three-dimensionally, that the sort of deathlessness that God has is of this latter sort: a life so completely deathless as to be able to assume being a shameful victimary corpse within itself, and become as such the source of life for others. So what is meant by the Resurrection as an impetus for moral life, is that we are inducted into beginning to live as if death were not, being able to befriend our mortality in all its extremities, extremities which include human victimhood in all its moral and physical dimensions. The outward and visible sign, if you like, of the resurrection in our lives, is the fear and stigma of death having become moot for us. And thereafter for our creativity, our longing for justice and flourishing, to have been unleashed into the beginnings of practical responses, by not having death as its circumscription.

Here again I think Girard's mimetic understanding of desire is very helpful in exploring how this works in our lives. As you may remember, what is central to that account is that *we desire according to the desire of another*. So, it is through the eyes of a model that an object acquires desirability. For instance, I who know nothing about art, find myself becoming friends with someone who is a connoisseur of fine art. As I spend time with her, her knowledge about, sensitivity towards, and enthusiasm for, fine art "rubs off on me", as we would say without thinking about it too exactly. And I find myself, on visits to museums and galleries, even where she is not present, appreciating and enjoying the works of art vastly more than I did before I knew her. In fact, what has happened is that I have started to see art through her eyes. It is not of course that I have put her on, like a mask, or a spacesuit, so that her eyes are on loan to me. It is the pattern of her desire which has reproduced itself in me, by my being drawn to imitate her, such that what it feels like at first is as if someone else were looking through my eyes and I am gradually coming to see what they see. Then, little by little, this becomes connatural to me, with my being scarcely aware of all the other pairs of eyes that have drawn me into my ever richer appreciation of the objects in question.

Well, it seems to me that this is the human and anthropological pattern that the resurrection has in our lives. If the model is God, and the object "creation", or everything that is, then the question becomes, "How do we learn to love, to desire, everything that is, in the same way that God does?" The difficulty is that God is not a model in any obvious sense. If we do not have a human model to imitate, one at our level, then we have no ability to desire according to God, and we will be left at the mercy of modelling each other's desire, while claiming that we desire according to a frightening sacred object who is in fact a projection of ourselves and of our fears and of our violence. What is traditionally called an "idol". We will be stuck, in fact, with that draw towards and repulsion from victims, a kind of unstable and two-faced fascination, which is what characterizes the archaic sacred.

However, what we have in Jesus' resurrection is a fully human set of eyes for whom death is not, a real human life story that is a living out at the anthropological level of the deathlessness of God. Because of this, that life is able to get alongside us and into us in the same way as the pattern of desire of the fine art connoisseur, and we start to be able to look at creation, at everything that is, through those same deathless eyes. The pattern of desire of the deathless one opens our eyes to what really is in the world, without us having to run away from, be run by, death. It becomes possible for us to be towards everything that is in the same way as the deathless one, and so to be creative and daring and imaginative without fear or hurry. The deathless one has opened up the possibility of our pattern of desire being

towards everything that is, in this quite specifically deathless way. And of course, everything that is actually looks
quite different if looked at with humanly deathless eyes.
Observation affects reality, as quantum physicists tell us.
Just as the reality of creation underwent a real change
when human consciousness was born, and anthropoids
started looking at everything round about them through
those hugely more powerful and dangerous things, human
eyes, so that same reality has been undergoing a further
change as, ever since Jesus' resurrection, reality has been
able to be observed from within itself by the deathless One
looking through fully human eyes into whose gaze we find
ourselves drawn.

OK, let's get back to the Samaritan. So far we've noticed
that he has been drawn towards the victim in a completely non-repulsed way, and that he is simply unmoved by
issues of death. So proximity is not a problem. But what is
in a sense just as interesting is that absence is not a problem either. As we carry on watching him, it seems that part
of this gut wrench which he is undergoing is sensed as a
tremendous privilege. He is finding himself on the inside
of the life of God! So he is quite unconcerned about sen-
sible limits to goodness. He is just delighted to find himself on the inside of this adventure. He doesn't try to palm
off the wounded one on the innkeeper. He seems to realize that he's found a centre to his life and activity that is
worth sticking with. Rather than saying to himself "How

little can I get away with and still be a decent person?" which is what I find myself thinking whenever I'm in an analogous situation, he seems to realize that he is being given something good by sharing the life of this victim. And this means that he *owns* the situation – makes it his own. And that of course means that he allows the victim to be the one who *owns him*.

However, this doesn't mean that he is now condemned, in some thoroughly unhealthy way, to be morbidly fixated on hanging in there with the victim, as though the victim needed to see him the whole time, or as though the only real sort of love or compassion were some perpetual and intense face to face with the vulnerable other. Nor does the Samaritan have any need to be seen to be doing good. Part of the privilege, on the inside of which he has discovered himself, is that he is able to take responsibility for the victim as a project over time, which means not being obsessively present, or obsessively absent. It means being able to be quite invisible while still caring for and looking after the victim, setting up intermediary agents and instruments who will be rewarded, and know they will be rewarded, for playing their part in his generosity.

This has involved him in making an open-ended commitment to the well-being of the victim without any fear that he would be limiting himself, be getting tied down, trapped, in a responsibility that would in some way diminish him. On the contrary, it is as though he has discovered with joy that he is going to be brought into being himself, become something much more, be added to enormously, precisely by his commitment to this precarious and unpredictable healing process. Being *owned* by the victim has turned out to be something much less panic-inducing, and much more spaciousness-creating than he would have thought possible.

And this, I think, is a second dimension to the process of beginning to live the life of the deathless one in the circumstances of contingent humanity. As death loses its power, so commitment to the flourishing of what is fragile and precarious becomes possible, and our relationship with time changes. I don't know about you, but pledging yourself in an open-ended manner to make good on the hospital expenses of a severely injured person without any guarantee of payback for yourself is mostly a terrifying possibility. What is to stop you being "taken to the cleaners" for everything you've got?

But what if time is not your enemy? If time is not your enemy, then what you achieve or don't achieve, whether you are "taken to the cleaners" or not, is secondary, and whatever you have will be for the flourishing of the weak one for as long as it takes, since you know that you will be *found there*. Being on the inside of the life of God looks like being decanted, by a generosity you didn't know you had in you, into making a rash commitment which makes a nonsense of death, of worry, and of the panic of time, because you know that you want to be found in loving proximity to what is weak and being brought into being. Wanting to be *found there* is a huge statement of joy at the power and gentleness of One for whom it is the apparently weak and futile things that are going to be enabled to be brought into being. Being given the daring to be able to lose yourself in being *found* there is recognized as a privilege to be greeted with praise.

This, I think, is what the Samaritan was discovering in his slow-burning, gentle and intelligent excitement, what St Paul would describe as "rightly reasoning worship".[50] That God is the One who brings into being *what is not*. And dwelling on the inside of the life of God means being prepared to lose sight of all the apparently important things that *are* and to give yourself away in extreme gentleness and tenderness towards that which is apparently not, and yet which is being brought into being out of the brink of nothingness by one not ashamed of mingling with the least important of all, one who has nowhere more important to be.[51]

So, what is Jesus doing now, what is it like to share his life? My own answer to that includes a tinge of jealousy: the Samaritan had it lucky in having God rush through his entrails like an express train. For most of us, the process of having our hearts turned from sacrifice to mercy is incredibly, incredibly painful. Since the more any of us loves, the

---

[50] Romans 12.1–2: λογικὴ λατρεία
[51] 1 Corinthians 1.22–29.

more any of us is given a heart of flesh, the more alive that heart becomes. And the more alive it becomes, the more raw and painful the world comes to seem, even if also much, much richer and more interesting.

4. John's testimony

Let us turn now to how St John deals with these matters. I'm going to put before you two different moments from the same discourse in St John's Gospel.

Let's look at this first:

> "A new commandment I give to you, that you love one another; even as I have loved you, that you also love one another."[52]

Now at first blush it appears that an instruction is given, and then its sense is unfolded by an example being proposed. We start with an instruction: that you love one another. However, just telling someone to love someone is not very useful, because left at that, it might simply be an injunction to strain your heart, or your will, towards someone, which you may or may not be able to do. So, an example is given, "as I have loved you", and this is supposed to add a little content to the demand that has been made. But we're still in the universe of moralistic instructions.

I'd like to suggest a slightly different approach. As I read it, the second half of the verse is an exact paraphrase of the first part, a repetition with the deepest meaning brought out. Jesus' *giving* a new commandment *consists in his doing*

---

[52] John 13.34.

something for his disciples. It is his doing something for them, loving them, in a quite concrete way, which is setting something in motion such that they are going to find themselves impelled and enabled to reproduce it for each other. So what he is doing, giving himself up in love for them, can equally well be described as the giving of a new commandment. Can you see how this is the reverse of a moralistic instruction? This gift of something done becomes a unique kind of commandment because it sets something in motion first, which then of itself stands as a summons inviting you in to reproduce it. It is as if Jesus were saying: "In order for you to be able to love each other, you need first to know what it is like to be loved, and as you sink into knowing the shape of my love for you, so you will be able to love each other."

I hope that you can see the difference: in one vision, something done for us becomes a defining source of our acting for others; in the other, we receive a moral injunction to do something huge but unclear. This difference fits straight in with the picture of being human that we've been looking at throughout this course: we are not individuals locked in on ourselves who must be told to do things; rather we are all little, imitative, mimetic interactors who do what we see done. In other words, we desire according to the desire of the other, as we've been learning throughout this course. The question is always: which other? When the other is Jesus, then, as we see Jesus doing for us, so we do. Love has a content from somewhere else, and the commandment is a commandment to imitate: "Even as I have loved you, so love one another."

This picture is filled out even more in our second chunk from St John:

> "This is my commandment, that you love one another as I have loved you. Greater love has no man than this, that a man lay down his life for his friends. You are my friends if you do what I command you." [53]

I hope you can see that there would be a glitch in this passage if we were to assume the moralistic "authority gives instruction" mode of teaching. Because in that mode, Jesus has friends, and lays down his life for them, and then commands them, who are already his friends, to do the same to others. However, that's not what the passage says! The passage presupposes that those for whom he gives his life *are not yet his friends*. On the contrary, he is opening up the possibility for them to become his friends by his doing something for them, on the inside of which they will then be able to find themselves as multipliers of exactly what he has done, which is how they will become his equals, his friends. They will become people who are going to be empowered to give themselves away, freely acting out of being insiders in something that has been opened up for them by someone who loved them.

In other words, the gift of creating this possibility for

---

[53] John 15.12–14.

his friends, and the commandment to create it *are the same thing*. There is no moralism here! There would be moralism if something were done, and as a result of it something were then commanded. That could indeed be a sort of emotional blackmail: "Look at me, I've done something for you, gone to so much trouble and suffering for you – now at least show that I have purchase on your heartstrings: do what I say." Instead of that, what we have is a personal invitation, so that each one of the disciples, which is each one of us, finds him- or herself being taken out of the realm of blind commandments into that sharing in equality of spirit which is friendship:

> *"No longer do I call you servants, for the servant does not know what his master is doing; but I have called you friends, for all that I have heard from my Father I have made known to you. You did not choose me, but I chose you and appointed you that you should go and bear fruit and that your fruit should abide; so that whatever you ask the Father in my name, he may give it to you. This I command you, to love one another."*[54]

Servants are told to do something, and if they don't understand why they should do it, they're told "You don't need to understand why, just do it, you're a servant. I, the Master, know why I want it done, and your ways are not my ways." Morals are often taught in this way! Friends, however, are chosen freely, and become trusted insiders on a level of equality with each other. They are not given com-

---

[54] John 15.15–17.

partmentalized tasks, but are entrusted with being imaginative, creative sharers in the whole project. As they share in a project, discovering for themselves the open-ended parameters which have been made available by the One who gave himself, so they will find that they are not only friends of the one who inaugurated the project, but brothers, heirs, the ultimate insiders, fully adopted into the life of the Son. Jesus makes it possible for us to share his desire at the level of equality, which is that of friendship. So we are enabled to desire as Jesus desires, according to the Father. Given that, it makes perfect sense to ask the Father for whatever we want, as if we were the Son, because we will in fact be becoming the Son, the ultimate insider in the life of God.

5. Paul, and receiving ourselves through the eyes of One who loves us

I hope that you can see what is central here, and this is essential to being inducted into the Christian faith: it presupposes that before we do anything, we are drawn in, by an initiative not our own, into becoming aware of what has been done for us. Do you see how quickly and easily we can jump over and forget phrases like "even as I have loved you", and remember only the "love one another" part? Yet it is our being loved *before we knew it* that has opened all this up. And that doesn't only mean that we are asked to remember *how much* we have been loved, as though it were in the first place a matter of emotional degree. It is more properly *the shape* of our being loved: that someone was prepared to occupy the place of victimage, and shame, and non-being, patiently and gently, out of love for us, long before we sensed how much we depended on such a thing. Or, as we read, once again, in John:

> For it was in **this** way that God loved the world: that he gave his only Son, that whoever believes in him should not perish but have eternal life.[55] (emphasis mine)

It is as we begin to get a sense of what it is like to be loved from that space of God's giving that we begin to be empowered, and impelled, to open it up for others.

And that, I think is actually the really difficult part of Christian morality: not what we do, but perceiving what has been done for us, becoming attentive to the one who is speaking us into being. This is because it is so much more difficult for us to allow ourselves to undergo something, to appreciate what we are finding ourselves on the inside of, and to allow ourselves to be stretched by it towards others, than it is to say "I haven't got the time for all that 'being loved' stuff – just tell me what to do."

---

[55] John 3.16. The majority of translations read "For God so loved the world", suggesting that the word "so" is a matter of emphasis, or psychological force – short for "so much". However, exactly the same words in Greek can be read to bring out a demonstrative sense: "God loved the world *so* – in just this way: namely, that he gave his only Son." I find this demonstrative sense more congruent with John's overall approach to revelation.

Yet this sinking into appreciation of being loved is no merely passive exercise. In fact it is usually through little acts of being stretched out towards others that we find ourselves becoming more aware of being loved, and the two moments, activity and undergoing, then enrich and inform each other.

In any case, I would like to offer you an exercise to enable you to sit over time in a sense of being on the receiving end of being loved. We're going to look at the famous passage from 1 Corinthians about love. This has acquired very particular associations for us owing to its use in weddings. So it tends to get linked to a particular account of love, and a particular moment of love, neither of which are bad things. But the passage is much richer than that. I'm going to read this passage not, if you like, as a piece of abstract moralism defining what love is, but as an invitation to dwell in what it looks like to be undergoing the presence of One who loves you. In other words, everything we've seen about Jesus the forgiving victim coming towards us, and our sitting in his regard.

> Love is patient and kind; love is not jealous or boastful; it is not arrogant or rude. Love does not insist on its own way; it is not irritable or resentful; it does not rejoice at wrong, but rejoices in the right. Love bears all things, believes all things, hopes all things, endures all things.[56]

You may remember from Essay 9, about prayer, that we

---

[56] 1 Corinthians 13.4–7.

looked at prayer as "sitting in the regard of the Other other". So here I'm asking you to allow yourselves to be looked at from the regard which Paul sets out.

What does it mean to realize that the One looking at me is doing so in a way that is patient? So, not looking at me in a hurry, impatient with my slowness and waywardness, needing me to get things right already. Able to take time, not needing to correct me yet; approaching me without edge, gently, in a way that is not out to get me, doesn't need to put me down – that is a kind regard. Those eyes are looking at me in a way that is not jealous, not in rivalry with me in any way, not disturbed if I'm having a good day, nor trying to manipulate me so as to get Brownie points. They aren't determined that I shouldn't have too good a time, since that will make me bigheaded, nor are they only wanting me to be successful so that they can feel successful through me, as though I were a means to their end.

They are genuinely hugely glad if I get something right, since they genuinely want my good, for no other purpose than that they like me. They are not arrogant, grasping things for themselves, marking off their turf and making me feel small by contrast, diminishing me with funny little names or labels that put me into a box and make me less. They have no need to put me down, by damning me with faint praise. Their praise is that of genuine delight in something equal with themselves.

What is it like to pick up that I am loved in this way?

"Love does not insist on its own way." What a very extraordinary thing to say! We are talking about the regard of God, the eyes of the Creator of the universe, looking at us, the one to whom we pray "Thy will be done." Yet the presence and regard of love is not in rivalry with our will. It is not someone trying to steamroller us, getting us to do something we find awful, trying to use us for a nefarious end. This presence of love has been prepared to put itself under us, and from that vulnerable place actually wants to join us in discovering *our* way, so that it's rejoicing and saying "Oh, that'll be fun! I wonder where she'll take it?" "Why would that be interesting? You really want to do that? OK, I'm with you!"

This regard is not irritable, or resentful – and don't we know what it is like to be held in an irritable or resentful regard! We're always too much, or too little, but we don't measure up. Whereas someone who is not irritable is saying "You know, you're just right! What fun it is to be with you! Are you having a wonderful time? That makes me *soooo* pleased!" Love doesn't rejoice at wrong – no *Schadenfreude* here, no sense of "I'm just waiting for you to trip up on some banana skin, and then you'll get your comeuppance. Your contentment now is just pride before a fall." This regard doesn't take any pleasure in my discomfiture, is not at all keen to see me getting things wrong "so that you'll learn", no smug satisfaction in my mistakes and my follies; rather it is just beaming when I get it right.

This regard, this presence of love, *bears all things*. What on earth is it like to bear all things? We can bear a certain amount of other people's sickness, other people's betrayals, their infidelities. All these things we can bear to a certain extent, though it's a great strain. So what is it like to discover that all my sickness, all my slowness, all my laziness, all my infidelities, are being borne by someone for whom I am still, just as I am, an exciting project?

This same love *believes all things*. It believes in me as an investment that despite all the evidence is going to give fruit. When I occasionally say something aspirational, that I would really like to be true, that I would really like to become and to achieve, but which is pretty unlikely given who I usually am, this regard doesn't say "Oh yeah, that's the kind of thing he says when he's in a good mood, but it's just a flash in the pan, we know what he's really like." But no, the regard of love takes me at my best, most aspirational, word, and believes in me over time so that the rest of me can catch up with the wild-card dream that I would have difficulty recognizing as myself. The regard of love says "It is going to be so much more fun to take you at your most daring, and make that true, rather than tease you and belittle you for having ideas above your station."

Believes all things, hopes all things, endures all things. So love doesn't take no for an answer, doesn't recognize things being closed off, shut down, instead it is constantly reimagining us as potential, as adventure. Love has already occupied the place of shame and rejection, of being a non-person in our midst, so it doesn't allow itself to be deflected by my hostility, looks past my anger, my resentment, my taking myself too seriously. Love is prepared to occupy the place of the loser, to endure loss, to be dead. Love not only puts up with all that, but while going through it all never loses sight of a me I often give up on, myself, a me by whom this lover wants to be enriched for ever.

This, all this, language of Paul's, is filling out dimensions of the regard of the Forgiving Victim in our midst. This is the space which Jesus has opened up for us so as to show us how God looks at us. It is as we find ourselves being looked at in this way, as we sink in to allowing this regard to tell us who we are, that we find ourselves impelled from within, contagiously, to do the same for others.

6. Epilogue: The "mmmmmm!" factor

Now, at the very end, we can go back to the beginning. Except that, as we have seen, in the Christian understanding, the beginning is not at some chronologically remote place in the distant past. The beginning has irrupted into what looks for us like the middle. It summons us into becoming insiders in what the beginning's really all about, dwellers whose being is given to us from what looks to us like a future that is opening itself into our midst, making us alive to it as it does so.

So let's go back to Genesis, which, as you remember from Essay 11, was brought to fruition in the Garden in John's Gospel. At the beginning of Genesis, God starts to make things, on different days. And after each day's work, God sees that it is good. On the sixth day God makes all the earth-bound living creatures (the aquatic and the winged variety had been made the day before). Again in God's regard, it is good. But then, before the sixth day fades, God seems to have a sudden seizure. Not content with the good things created that day, God decides to double down on the earth-bound creatures and creates humanity in God's image and likeness. Having pulled off this feat, and just before resting, God looks at everything. This time God does not merely notice that it is good. Now it looks to God to be *very* good.

Of course, those words have been read countless times over the last two and a half millennia. And each generation reads them according to our preconceptions. One of the ways of reading them has been to see this passage as being a narrative way by which God declared creation to be intrinsically, and objectively good, a kind of philosophical remark to ensure proper morals flowing from the order of creation. I wonder whether it wouldn't be closer to the much more personal, relational way in which the Hebrew texts tell us of such things if we were to look at the passage slightly differently. It seems to me that what we have in verbal form is God purring with contentment and delight

at what God sees coming into being: "Mmmmm, I like it."
It is the apple of God's eye. And then on the sixth day, having indulged his adventurous eccentricity by bringing
humans into being: "Mmmmmm, I *really* like it."

I use the word "like" deliberately, since we usually use
the word "love" when talking about how God imagines the
world. But the word "love" often enough has control-freak
associations, such that people can tell us that they love us,
and that is why we must become something else. In other
words, their "love" serves as an excuse for not actually *liking* the person in front of them. One of the reasons that I
prefer the word "like" is that it is much more difficult to lie
about. We can tell whether someone likes us or not. Their
body language and way of being present to us speak more
loudly than their words. Someone who *likes* you enjoys
being with you, alongside you, wants to share your time
and your company, doesn't control you, but is curious to
see where you're going to take things, and will delight with
you in wherever it goes.

So, with that "mmmmmm" of God, the *goodness of
everything that is* is not a decree, or a definition. It is a relationship of *really being liked* by the one who is bringing it
into being, and whose regard is out-of-himself delight in
what we are and may become. What we've been looking at
in this course is how that regard, of *liking* us, came alive
for us in our midst, occupying the space in our world, the
victim space, whose existence is our sad tribute to our

being unable to believe that we are liked. This coming into our midst was to try to prove to us that most difficult of truths: that in the midst of all the mess, the fear, the violence and the hatred which abound in our world, we are *liked* irrepressibly, lyrically, chucklingly, light-heartedly, wastefully, as we are. A word of morality flowing from a heart that does not like is indeed part of vanity. Because the creating and the liking are the same thing. And those liking eyes, made even more alive for us by having shared our story from within, look at us and say "Be of good cheer, I have overcome the world."[57]

---

[57] John 16.33.

Scriptural References

Book Four

Colossians 1.15–20, p 482

Colossians 3.1–5, p 523

1 Corinthians 1.22–29, p 550

1 Corinthians 6.12, p 465

1 Corinthians 8.6, p 482

1 Corinthians 13.4–7, p 557

Deuteronomy 6.5, p 528

Ephesians 1.3–14, p 482

Genesis 1.1–2, p 498

Genesis 2.7, p 506

Genesis 3.19, p 498

Genesis 3.2–3, p 504

Hebrews 1.1–3, p 481

Hosea 6.6, p 540

Isaiah 55.1–3, p 423

Isaiah 66.7–8, p 516

John 1.1–2, p 482

John 3.16, p 556

John 5.44, p 474

John 13.34, p 551

John 15.12–14, p 553

John 15.15–17, p 554

John 16.7–11, p 496

John 16.20–22, p 515
John 16.33, p 564
John 19.26–27, p 514
John 19.34b, p 516
John 20.1–23, p 503
John 20.17, p 516
John 20.22, p 506
Leviticus 19.18, p 528
Leviticus 19.33–34, p 532
Luke 2, p 511
Luke 6.28, p 419
Luke 8.19–21, p 512
Luke 10.25–37, pp 527-540
Luke 12.1b–2, p 474
Luke 18.1–8, pp 415-417
Luke 22.42, p 498
Luke 22.44, p 499
Luke 23.43–46, pp 499-500
Mark 7.13, p 475
Mark 8.33, p 407
Mark 10.29–31, p 519
Matthew 5.44–45, p 420
Matthew 6.1–4, pp 408
Matthew 6.5–6, p 411
Matthew 6.6, p 401
Matthew 6.7–8, p 400
Matthew 6.7–8, p 424

Matthew 6.9–15, pp 426-433
Matthew 20.25b–28, p 473
Matthew 23.4, p 475
Matthew 23.8, 10b, p 475
Matthew 23.24, p 475
Romans 6.3–14, p 523
Romans 8.18–23, p 502
Romans 8.22–27, pp 404-405
Romans 12.1–2, p 550
1 Thessalonians 5.19, p 477

Video References

The essays in Book Four correspond to Unit Four of the video curriculum. Essay Nine has been divided into two videos, Essay Ten into three videos, Essay Eleven into three videos and Essay Twelve into two videos for a total of ten videos.

Essay Section	Pages	Corresponding Video
Essay 9 – Prayer: Getting inside desire's shift in us		
Intro. & Sections 1-4	pp 397-415	Part 4 Session 1 Video - _The working of desire_
Sections 5-8	pp 415-433	Part 4 Session 2 Video - _The Our Father_
Essay 10 – The portal and the halfway house: Spacious imagination and aristocratic belonging		
Introduction, 1-2, through paragraph ending "The halfway house, like the Church, is an effective sign of a draw from beyond itself that is empowering its residents into becoming creators of society."	pp 435-448	Part 4 Session 3 Video - _The restaurant and the halfway house_
Remainder of 2-5	pp 448-461	Part 4 Session 4 Video - _The portal and the Embassy_
Sections 6-7	pp 462-479	Part 4 Session 5 Video - _The Banquet_

Essay Section	Pages	Corresponding Video

Essay 11 – A little family upheaval

Intro. & Sections 1-3	pp 481-497	Part 4 Session 6 Video - *A little family upheaval*
Sections 4-5	pp 497-508	Part 4 Session 7 Video - *The beginning in the middle*
Section 6	pp 508-520	Part 4 Session 8 Video - *The grandeur in the everyday*

Essay 12 – Neighbors and Insiders: What's it like to dwell in a non-moralistic commandment?

| Intro. & Sections 1-3 ending with the paragraph that ends, "And how victimhood is an ineluctable reality in our species." | pp 521-542 | Part 4 Session 9 Video - *Neighbors and insiders: The Good Samaritan* |
| Remainder of 3-6 | pp 542-564 | Part 4 Session 10 Video - *Neighbors and insiders: From sacrifice to mercy* |

Glossary of Terms

Some terms and phrases are used in ways which may be unfamiliar to you. Please note that these are not dictionary definitions, but quick guides to help easy understanding.

Bibliolatry – the default Protestant error is "bibliolatry," making an idol of the Bible.

Ecclesiolatry – the default Catholic error is "ecclesiolatry," making an idol of the Church.

Evil – There is nothing evil in God, and any attribution of evil to God prevents us from trusting God wholeheartedly. Genuinely evil confluences of relationships and events really do occur, but we are wise to be very sparing in our use of the word. In fact, the thing about evil is the more we try to define it and face it, the more fascinating it becomes, and the more we turn into the object of our fascination. Any of us can see this when we see someone we know get fixated on an enemy or rival, and then, without realizing it, become more and more like them until they are mirror images of each other. The real force in the universe is love, not evil. Love seeks to rescue us from our tendency to enclose ourselves in ever-smaller spaces through fear, and instead to bring us into a flourishing aliveness.

Narcissism of Minor Differences – the way in which there is much greater chance of rivalry between people who are very much alike, than between people who are quite different from each other. A fury is often triggered when we encounter an "other" who is uncomfortably like us, bringing out elements of what we don't like about ourselves, but don't realize it. For instance, to understand the story told in Luke 10, it is helpful to understand that the Samaritans worshipped the same God as their Jewish neighbors, with a slightly different, but overlapping, set of Scriptures. They didn't acknowledge Jerusalem as a sacred center, worshipping instead on Mount Gerizim. So Jews and Samaritans, owing to their extreme proximity and similarity, were a perpetual reproach to each other, sources of reciprocal moral infuriation.

Secondariness – the relaxing sense we can sometimes glimpse of "it doesn't all start with, or gravitate around, me". So, the more time we spend in the presence of "I AM," we catch a glimpse of ourselves as real, contingent, alive; we discover that we are held in being by something prior to us, something that is not at the same level as ourselves or in rivalry with anything. This is not a form of diminishment, or being put down, but an accurate and objective sense of createdness, something which can in fact be relaxed into with gratitude.